John Ruskin, Preacher
And Other Essays

John Ruskin, Preacher
And Other Essays

BY

LEWIS HERBERT CHRISMAN

Essay Index Reprint Series

BOOKS FOR LIBRARIES PRESS
FREEPORT, NEW YORK

First Published 1921

Reprinted in this Series 1966, 1969

STANDARD BOOK NUMBER:

8369-1328-0

LIBRARY OF CONGRESS CATALOG CARD NUMBER:

67-22086

CONTENTS

CONTENTS

I

JOHN RUSKIN, PREACHER

ALTHOUGH he wore no black Geneva gown
and never stood behind the sacred desk, John
Ruskin all of his days was a golden-mouthed,
burning-hearted, spiritually minded preacher of
the truths of God. The Rev. W. P. Paterson,
a Scottish theologian, recently said, "During
the bygone century it may be doubted if the
ornaments of the Christian pulpit did as much
as lay preachers like Carlyle and Ruskin to
quicken the social conscience and to commend lofty ideals in the various departments
of secular life and labor." Like the melancholy prophet of Judah's shadowed days,
Ruskin was "valiant for truth." For over
twenty years he was preeminently a critic of
art. But he was no dilettante defender of
that pictorial putrescence which is sometimes
foisted upon a gullible public by depraved
purveyors of vileness which they miscall art.
Ruskin was the unfailing champion of the
things which are honest and just and pure
and lovely and of good report. His dominant

7

concern was with the mighty truths of human nature upon which the laws of both art and life are based. In one of his key sentences he tells us "that the manual arts are as accurate exponents of ethical states as other modes of expression: first, with absolute precision, of that of the workman, and then with precision disguised by many distorting influences, of that of the nation to which it belongs."

In the gospel according to Ruskin, we are taught that there can be no real beauty which does not emanate from beauty of soul. The character of a people is both the cause and result of its art. By their fruits ye shall know them. A noble art can exist only as the fruit of a noble soul. It cannot be produced by a besotted, materialized, shriveled-souled people. Neither is art without its reaction upon life. Ruskin's father would not allow his son to look at an impure or careless painting. If a people are compelled to live in constant contact with that which is common and vile, the very warp and woof of their lives is bound to be coarsened. A real interpreter of art must be an interpreter of life as well. Ruskin as he battled for purity and sincerity in painting and sculpture and architecture, was fighting a good fight for noble ideals of thought and action. "Be a good man," says Carlyle, "and there'll be one rascal less." Ruskin again and again teaches the same lesson. Whatever his theme, before he is through with it he is sure to make it a discussion of the conduct of life.

In Traffic he says: "The first, and last, and closest trial question to any living creature is, 'What do you like?' Tell me what you like and I'll tell you what you are. Go out into the street and ask the first man or woman you meet what their taste is; and if they answer candidly, you know them, body and soul." He most strenuously objected to being regarded as a "respectable architectural man-milliner," dispensing the latest information as to the "newest and sweetest thing in pinnacles." This great prophet of reality was not satisfied with mere doing of the right, but he insisted on the necessity of loving the right. His Scottish mother had so indoctrinated him with the spirit of the New Testament that he well understood that there is that which goes beyond verbose piety and Pharisaic legalism. He never failed to emphasize the dominance of the inner life. He knew that above all else the cup must be pure within. He writes: "Would you paint a great picture? be a good man. Would you carve a perfect statue? be a pure man. Would you enact a wise law?

be a just man." But Ruskin was no effete
preacher of a nebulous ethical culture. He
is quoted as saying that his life was dedicated
not to "the study of the beautiful in face or
flower, in landscape or gallery, but to an interpretation of the truth and beauty of Jesus
Christ."

But when Ruskin was about forty years of
age he saw a new vision. He had been growing more and more sensitive to the hammer
blows struck by Carlyle in Sartor Resartus,
in Chartism and Past and Present. In all of
his efforts to secure practical application of
his art teaching, he was impeded by unjust
and revolting social and industrial conditions.
England, full of wealth, with its multifarious
produce, with supply for every human want,
was, as has been said with tragic truth, "dying
of inanition." Two million of her workers,
"the cunningest, the strongest, and the willingest our earth ever had," sat in workhouses
and in the poor-law prisons. In counties of
which the green fields were dotted with herds
and flocks, the farm laborer did not taste
meat from one year to another. On many a
night there set out from London a vehicle
loaded to the breaking point with "two-legged
live stock": London foundlings being disposed
by contract to employers of labor in northern

factories. In the mines miserable women, naked to the waist, crawled through narrow passages drawing after them cars laden with coal. On the one hand was a careless, blatant, vulgar luxury and on the other a sullen, hopeless, defiant poverty. "It is no time for the idleness of metaphysics or the entertainment of the arts," said Ruskin.

His ever-deepening conviction that the very fountains of English life were impure impelled him to turn his back upon the fields in which he had labored with joy and honor to become a veritable voice crying in the wilderness. Unto This Last, the work which marks his transition, first appeared in the Cornhill Magazine. These papers were a stone thrown into the standing pool of contemporary economic thought. Political economy had indeed become the "dismal science." It was committing the cardinal sin of substituting logic for life. In the minds of many the conclusions of the "Manchester School" were the law delivered once for all. Ruskin's onslaught against economic orthodoxy won for him the excoriations of thousands. He exchanged laudation for obloquy. The articles were unpopular to such an extent that Thackeray, at that time editor of the Cornhill, was compelled to limit the projected series to four articles. Ruskin's

"rattle-brained radicalism" consisted merely in
trying to apply the teachings of Christianity to
the industrial conditions of his own day. It
is altogether possible that he was sometimes
profoundly mistaken. He was, moreover, ex-
treme in many of his statements. The ability
to coo as gently as a dove was not a
notable characteristic of Ruskin. But as we
read Unto This Last to-day and view its
teachings from the vantage ground of another
generation, it is difficult for us to understand
why its teachings were received with so many
"showers of oil of vitriol."

For John Ruskin the die had been cast.
Henceforth he was, like the knights of other
days, to give his life to redressing human
wrong. The interpreter of art had become a
social reformer. This change of viewpoint had
a most marked influence upon his literary
style. He deliberately pruned the overrich
eloquence of his earlier days; with little loss of
its pristine beauty it became more concise,
well-knit, and muscular. As the years passed
by he preached with ever intenser vehemence
and skill. To that which had been but a
thunderous roar in Carlyle he gave precision,
reality, and convicting power. There is a
danger which not all writers about him have
avoided: of fixing too great a gulf between the

two phases of Ruskin's literary life. It must
be remembered that in the years when he was
distinctively an art critic he was also a prophet
of social betterment, and also that in the
latter part of his life he delivered some of his
most luminous lectures on art.

If Ruskin had simply said that it was wrong
for a man of superior strength to strangle his
weaker neighbor out of hate for him, everybody would have agreed. But he went further
and contended that it was just as sinful for
an individual of superior shrewdness to take
advantage of some less gifted brother. It is
to be most earnestly hoped that such teaching
would not be found revolutionary to-day either
in England or in America. A reading of the
history of our own country in the decades
immediately following the Civil War, when it
seemed as though many of our national leaders
were willing to lower their ethical standards
in order to fill their coffers, impresses upon us
the fact that within the last twenty years we
have passed through a renaissance of righteousness. To the modern man of our generation
the social message of Ruskin is not especially
startling. "The survival of the fittest" is not
the law of an industrialism which is Christian. Ruskin says: "You would be indignant
if you saw a strong man walk into a theater

or lecture room and calmly choose the best place, take his feeble neighbor by the shoulder and turn him out of it into the back seats or the street. You would be equally indignant if you saw a stout fellow thrust himself up to a table where some hungry children were being fed and reach his arm over their heads and take the bread from them. But you are not the least indignant if, when a man has stoutness of thought and swiftness of capacity, and instead of being long-armed only has the much greater gift of being long-headed, you think it perfectly just that he should use his intellect to take the bread out of the mouths of all the other men in the town who are in the same trade with him; or use his breadth of sweep and sight to gather some branch of the commerce of the country into one great cobweb of which he is himself to be the central spider, making every thread vibrate with the points of his claws, commanding every avenue with the facets of his eyes. You see no injustice in this."

Strength is never an excuse for tyranny. "We that are strong ought to bear the infirmities of the weak," said the great apostle to the Gentiles. There are times when unrestrained competition may be nothing more or less than flagrant robbery. Christianity is pre-

eminently social. In Sur la Propriété, by
Emile de Laveleye, the author gives expression
to this significant thought: "There is a social
order which is the best. Necessarily it is not
always the present order. Else why should we
seek to change the latter? But it is that order
which ought to exist to realize the greatest
good for humanity. God knows it and wills
it. It is for man to discover and establish it."
Ruskin was one of the pioneers in the search
for the best social order. Many have followed in his footsteps. The splendid literature,
prophetic of an era of brotherhood and
justice given to us by forward-looking leaders of modern thought, belongs to the heritage
which has come to our generation from John
Ruskin, preacher of social righteousness and
justice.

Ruskin had no language too scathing with
which to denounce the nominal religion of
materialized men and women. In his day, as
in ours, ecclesiasticism and religion were not
always synonymous terms. There were those
who sat in high seats in the temples who worshiped not God but the "Goddess of Getting-on," or "Britannia of the Market." Again
and again with consummate eloquence and unrestrained irony he denounced that miscalled
Christianity which expressed itself in barren

formalism or in a succession of emotions unre-
lated to actual living. He emphasized the old
truth, "No man can serve two masters." A
man cannot endure as seeing Him who is
invisible and at the same time bow before the
golden shrine of the "Goddess of Getting-on."
Christianity is not something remote from life.
It is that which can permeate, transform, and
glorify every sphere and every task. A certain English lord is quoted as saying, "I respect
Christianity as much as any man, but I object
when they try to make it interfere with a
man's private life." In his book New Worlds
for Old, H. G. Wells tells of a transaction by
which the capital of a railroad was swollen from
forty million to nearly one hundred and twenty-
three millions to cover an expenditure in im-
provements of twenty-two and a half millions.
It is unfortunately often the case that finan-
ciers who mulct the public in this fashion
are members of orthodox communion, and make
a point of being regarded as religious. Ruskin
objected to formal piety being a cloak for
predatory industrialism. In The Crown of
Wild Olives we find this sentence, striking in
its simple truth: "The one Divine work—the
one ordered sacrifice—is to do justice."
    Ruskin was not a socialist, although many of
the ideas of modern socialism have sprung

from seed which he planted. We must also admit that he was not entirely successful in his effort to apply his social teaching to the life of his generation. Yet it must be remembered that seldom indeed do the prophet and the executive dwell in the same tenement of clay. We have no particular reason for believing that Amos of Tekoa would have been the ideal man to organize a new social system; we find it slightly difficult to picture John the Baptist in the guise of an ecclesiastical organizer. Ruskin was an artist and a preacher and not an administrator. Of him it can be said as of the parish priest in Chaucer's Canterbury Tales:

"But Cristes lore, and his apostles twelve,
He taughte, but first he folwed it him-selve."

Carlyle and Spencer, in the seclusion of their libraries, talked most passionately, and often most wisely, about the regeneration of modern society. They lived laborious, strenuous, silent, useful lives, but they never stirred one finger to change the conditions against which they fulminated. No one blames them; they had other work. But Ruskin, by far the most productive of our modern English writers, toiled "like a curate or missionary in some crowded parish," caring for the bodies, the

minds, and the souls of his weaker brethren.
Frederic Harrison has well said, "The first life
of John Ruskin was the life of a consummate
teacher of art and master of style; the second
life was the life of priest and evangelist."

Unlike certain modern preachers of the social
gospel, Ruskin did not minimize individual
righteousness. In valiant, hard-hitting English
he denounces the godlessness of a people of
jaded moral sense. His sarcastic version of
the Ten Commandments is a veritable philippic
against subtle hypocrisy:

"Thou shalt have gods of self and ease and
pleasure before me. Thou shalt worship thine
own imaginations as to house and goods and
business, and bow down and serve them.
Thou shalt remember the Sabbath day, to see
to it that all its hours are given to sloth and
lounging and stuffing the body with rich foods,
leaving the children of sorrow and ignorance
to perish in their sodden misfortune. Thou
shalt kill and slay men by doing as little as
possible thyself, and squeezing as much as
possible out of others. Thou shalt look upon
loveliness in womanhood to soil it with im-
purity. Thou shalt steal daily; the employer
from the servant and the servant from the
employer, and the devil take the hindmost.
Thou shalt get thy livelihood by weaving a

great web of falsehoods and sheathing thyself
in lies. Thou shalt covet thy neighbor's house
to possess it for thyself; thou shalt covet his
office and his farm, his goods and his fame,
and everything that is his. And to crown all
these laws the devil has added a new command-
ment—thou shalt hate thy neighbor as thou
dost hate thyself."

Ruskin, above all else, endeavored to avoid
expressing banal nothingness in eloquent language. He was mostly exceedingly concrete in
his denunciations of evil doing. As he grew
older he was dominated more and more by a
sense of wrongs to be righted. The thought
that in the midst of sorrow, suffering, wretched-
ness, and sin those whose talents and opportunities should have made them the real leaders of their people, were giving their days to
game-preserving and to vapid society made
him grow bitter. To him sin was no empty
abstraction. His very soul was thrilled by
what Carlyle called "a divine rage against
falsity." His stern words like a flame of fire
descended upon grossness, luxury, and mammonism. With something of the spirit and
power of the Hebrew prophets he stood for
duty rather than privilege, character rather
than possession, and ideals rather than ma-
terials. He knew that a transformed society

could consist only of regenerated men and
women. He knew of the battles between the
powers of light and the powers of darkness
which are fought in every human heart.
"Every faculty of man's soul, and every in-
stinct of it by which he is meant to live, is
exposed to its own special form of corruption:
and whether within man, or in the external
world, there is a power or condition of tempta-
tion which is perpetually endeavoring to reduce
every glory of his soul, and every power of
his life, to such corruption as is possible to
them." Much as he stressed social betterment, he realized that it is futile without
individual salvation. The truth, "Man is more
than meat," stands at the very heart of his
teaching. It was borne in upon him that the
making of human souls is the most important
manufacture in which a nation's energies could
be engaged. He hoped to rouse England to
a sense of her failure and to cause her to put
first things first. He said, "In some far-away
and yet undreamt-of hour I can imagine that
England may cast all thoughts of possessive
wealth back to the barbaric nations among
whom they first arose; and that while the
sands of the Indus and the adamant of Golconda may yet stiffen the housings of a charger
and flash from the turbans of a slave, she, as

a Christian mother, may at last be able to
attain the virtues of a heathen one and be
able to lead forth her sons saying, 'These are
My Jewels.' "

It is much easier to find in the writings of
Ruskin eloquent, helpful, soul-stirring, ideal-
kindling sermons than it is to find the out-
lines of his theology. He was far from being
a systematic thinker. It is hard to compress
into stern syllogisms the fine frenzy of the
poet. Until he was forty years of age his
theology was the softened Calvinism which he
inherited from his parents. He was in Oxford
in the days of the Tractarian movement, but
was absolutely untouched by it. He was always more interested in conclusions than he
was in the processes by which they were
attained. But about 1860 he became very
much unsettled in regard to the thought
foundations of his religious life. Had this
inevitable readjustment come earlier, it would
have been much less painful. To analyze his
later theology would be difficult. But we do
know that he became fired with an even
greater passion for righteousness and justice.
His love of good became more fervent and his
hatred of evil more intense. With even greater
frequency he recurred to Christ and his teachings. In the introduction to his Notes on the

Construction of Sheepfolds he remarks, "Many persons will probably find fault with me for publishing opinions which are not new; but I shall bear the blame contentedly believing that opinions on this subject could hardly be just if they were not eighteen hundred years old." His theology, unsystematic as it may be, is distinctively Christocentric.

Few writers quote the Bible so frequently or so effectively. Some of his noblest passages are almost biblical paraphrases. The last paragraph of the second paper of Sesame and Lilies is a notable example of this. In Præterita he gives a list of the chapters which his mother with the greatest exactness compelled him to memorize. He says that in this way his mother "established my soul in life," and adds the following comment: "And truly, though I have picked up the elements of a little further knowledge—in mathematics, meteorology, and the like, in after life—and owe not a little to the teaching of many people, this maternal installation of my mind in the property of chapters, I count very confidently the most precious, and, on the whole, the one essential part of all my education." To say the least, such a statement is not without profound pedagogical significance. It, moreover, helps us to understand the dominating forces in the life and writings of Ruskin. He was most emphatically a biblical preacher.

He has been criticized for his unrestrained language of denunciation. He speaks of London, the home of Chaucer and Milton, the city which Johnson loved and Turner painted, as "that great foul city, rattling, growling, smoking, stinking, a ghastly heap of fermenting brickwork, pouring out poison at every pore." In common with Carlyle, Ruskin, it must be admitted, excelled in the richness of his vocabulary of vituperation But in the Book which Ruskin knew above all others we find that the major and minor prophets spoke words of undiluted strength, and that Peter and Paul were not afraid to speak out. Then, too, there was One greater than prophet or apostle who denounced the formalistic, hypocritical scribes and Pharisees in words so fraught with fury that language almost breaks down beneath their weight. To hate wrong is the mark of a real Christian. A man tremendously in earnest in the presence of "ignorance, animality, and brutemindedness" does not keep silent or speak in accents of cowardly mildness. In no age does the prophet of the living God quail before enthroned evil.

The heart of John Ruskin was strangely warmed within him. Few men have been so

impressed with the high seriousness of life.
He believed that the issues of life and death
depended upon the gospel. "Precious indeed
those thirty minutes by which the teacher
tries to get at the separate hearts of a thousand
men, to convince them of all their weaknesses,
to shame them for all their sin, to warn them
of all their dangers, to try them by this way
and that, to stir the hard fastenings of the
doors where the Master himself has stood and
knocked, yet none opened, and to call at the
openings of those dark streets where Wisdom
herself hath stretched forth her hands and no
man regarded. Thirty minutes to raise the
dead in." Nowhere do we find a better sum-
mary of what for over half a century, misunderstood, assailed, ridiculed, and thwarted,
John Ruskin tried to do. He was a preacher
of the life abundant, a soldier beneath the
ensign of the King of kings.

II

JONATHAN EDWARDS

Most great men live in the future, but Jonathan Edwards was the child of the past. Most emphatically he was not one of the great radicals who overthrow long-entrenched systems and lay new foundations upon which after generations can build. On the contrary, he used his transcendent genius in a vain attempt to revitalize a dead philosophy and a fast-dying creed. But in spite of this, by the dominating force of a mighty intellect, he towers to-day, among our American thinkers, like a colossus.

In the early days of the New England theocracy the clergy were the lords of the land. The New England parson in his black Geneva cloak and close-fitting black velvet cap was an autocrat of the autocrats. He ruled his little world with a scepter of iron. From the high pulpit in the cold and cheerless meetinghouse he preached the militant, unyielding gospel of John Knox and John Calvin with an almost oracular authority. Woe to the unlucky wight who dared to criticize the Lord's anointed. His tongue was in danger of a cleft stick. In church and state the preacher reigned supreme. But Edwards, born in 1703, came into the world just in time to see, as a young man, the Mathers, son and father, fight their last losing battle for the old faith and the old theocracy. It would not be altogether amiss to say that Jonathan Edwards was the successor of Cotton Mather as the champion of the iron-clad Calvinism of an earlier day.

Dr. O. W. Holmes used to refer to himself as a "Brahman of the Brahmans." Edwards also could boast of a priestly ancestry. His father, Timothy Edwards, was for sixty years minister of the East Parish of Windsor, Connecticut, and his maternal grandfather, Solomon Stoddard, of Northampton, was one of the ecclesiastical giants of his day. Perhaps it is not altogether an unmixed evil that the usual anecdotes, both real and fabulous, of Edwards's youthful days are lacking. All signs, however, point to extraordinary intellectual precocity. At the age of twelve he wrote a letter refuting with some skill the idea of the materiality of the soul. The same year he produced an elaborate account of the habits of the spider based on his own observation. At thirteen he entered Yale College, which had been founded about fifteen years before. In speaking of the foundation of this ancient New England institution President Hadley says: "Yale College was founded after a fashion, at the beginning of the eighteenth century along the north shore of Long Island Sound. For many years it was difficult to say what it was and where it belonged." During Edwards's college days his Alma Mater was somewhat of a pilgrim and a stranger on the face of the earth, moving from one town to another every year or so. But such as the college was, Edwards followed it faithfully and remained with it two years as a special student after he received his first degree in 1719. And, in addition, for two years (1724–1726) he was a tutor at Yale and, according to Dr. Stiles, was one of the "pillar" tutors. We read elsewhere that he filled and sustained his office with great ability, dignity, and honor.

As we turn the meager pages which tell of his earlier years we sometimes feel a human curiosity to know more. Was he ever a real boy when he ought to have been such, or was he simply a miniature old man? What had he in common with the rollicking student of to-day? Was his soul so warped by a harsh theology and his mind so debauched with

intellectuality that his sympathies were narrow
and his life cabined, cribbed, confined? Sometimes we are inclined to give one answer and
sometimes another, but at the best we can
do little more than idly speculate. In regard
to the inner life of Jonathan Edwards, however,
we do not have to grope long in darkness,
and when we know the facts of a man's soul-
life we cannot but know what manner of a
man he was among his fellows.

We read in his diary these significant words:
"On Jan. 12, 1723, I made a solemn dedication
of myself to God and wrote it down, giving
up myself and all that I had to God, to be for
the future in no respect my own; to act as
one that had no right to himself in any respect
and solemnly vowed to take God for my whole
portion and felicity, looking on nothing else
as any part of my happiness, nor acting as if
it were; and his law for the constant rule of
my obedience, engaging to fight with all my
might against the world, the flesh, and the
devil, to the end of my life." Nor was he
content with a devotion to simply theological
abstractions. He made resolution after resolution affecting every phase of his life. His
writings during the Yale period show him to
be a high-minded young man fighting, as
many a youth has done, the old battle between

the promptings of his heart and the teachings
of the faith of his fathers. As we read his
resolutions we see that one of his incentives
for piety was the not particularly noble thought
of the advantages which it would win for
him in the next world. The ascetic tendency
which was such a dominant characteristic of
New England life finds full expression in his
earlier writing. Some of his resolutions for
self-mortification could have been written by
a Saint Simeon Stylites. These characteristics
in the young New Englander are not hard to
explain in the light of his environment, but
other phases of his intellectual life have proved
almost inexplicable to his biographers.

Now and then we find in his early writings
paragraphs which could have well been written
by the "God-intoxicated" Spinoza. There is
little in common between the teachings of
the inspired Hebrew and the harsh Augustinian
Calvinism with which Edwards had been indoctrinated from his earliest youth. The fact
that Edwards, who had never read Spinoza,
was able to strike such a deep philosophical
note is additional evidence of the transcendent
genius of this wonderful boy. Yet Spinoza
was not the philosopher with whom Edwards
had the most in common. The writings of
his early twenties are strongly tinctured with

Berkeleyan idealism. As to whether he had ever read the works of the English philosopher has long been a mooted question. But within recent years the best authorities have lent the weight of their influence to the negative side. Consequently, if we accept their dictums, we have another illustration of the marked originality which characterized Edwards in the days of his young manhood. Nevertheless, it matters little whether or not he read Berkeley. At this period of his life he showed a depth of insight which makes us wonder what his contribution to the world of thought would have been had he devoted his life to philosophy. Yet even then he was preeminently not a metaphysician but a theologian. Years afterward, in speaking of the intellectual and spiritual battles of these days, he said: "From my childhood up my mind had been full of objections against the doctrine of God's sovereignty in choosing whom he would to eternal life and rejecting whom he pleased, leaving them eternally to perish and be everlastingly tormented in hell. It used to appear like a horrible doctrine to me. I remember the time very well when I seemed to be convinced and fully satisfied as to this sovereignty of God, and his justice in thus eternally disposing of men according to his sovereign pleasure, but never could give an account how or by what means I was thus convinced, not in the least imagining at the time, nor a long time after, that there was any extraordinary influence of God's Spirit in it, but only that now I saw further, and my mind apprehended the justice and reasonableness of it. However, my mind rested in it, and it put an end to all these cavils and questioning." In speaking of these words Dr. Allen says: "So Edwards entered into the heritage of his fathers and made the Puritan consciousness his own. There are traces of an inward rebellion which was suppressed. There is reason to believe that his success was not so complete as he fancied in eradicating his earlier thought. But the critical point of the transition is not explained. It is buried out of sight in silence and darkness."

From this time forth Jonathan Edwards stood in the front ranks of the champions of the old New England theology. In 1727 he was ordained at Northampton as copastor with his distinguished grandfather, the Rev Solomon Stoddard. To the work of this parish, where he remained for twenty-three years, he gave the best of his life. He was anything but a lazy preacher. He was extremely conscientious in the performance of his parish duties, and he made it a point to spend thirteen hours a day in his study. His solitary walks and rides were his sole diversion. Even then the busy mind did not rest. He often came home from his journeys with his coat decorated with small pieces of paper on which he had written the thoughts which had come to him while away from his study.

He was never a popular preacher in the ordinary sense of the word. His sermons are, of course, limited by the arbitrary homiletical divisions of his day. They are most appallingly logical and, to put it very mildly, their theology does not attract the twentieth-century reader. Yet the fire of life and reality still burns in them. His most widely heralded sermon is his famous fire-and-brimstone production, "Sinners in the Hands of an Angry God." But, contrary to the generally accepted belief, this is not one of his characteristic productions. He was not a brazen-lunged Boanerges thundering forth edicts of terror against a lost world. Neither the man nor the preacher can be judged by his theology. His latest biographer says, "He was at his best and greatest, most original and creative when he described the divine love." He was a poet as well as a theologian. In one of his sermons we read: "When we behold the fragrant rose and lily, we see His love and purity. So the green trees and fields and singing of birds are the emanations of His infinite joy and benignity. The loveliness and naturalness of trees and vines are shadows of His beauty and loveliness." His favorite text was, "I am the Rose of Sharon and the Lily of the Valley," and his favorite words were "sweet and bright."

New England asceticism did not mean celibacy. A few months after his ordination Edwards brought to Northampton as his bride the beautiful and saintly Sarah Pierpont. Several years before, about her, he had written the following memorable passage:

"They say that there is a young lady in New Haven who is beloved of that great Being who made and rules the world and that there are certain seasons in which this great Being, in some way or other invisible, comes to her and fills her mind with exceeding sweet delight, and that she hardly cares for anything except to meditate on him; that she expects after a while to be received up where he is, to be raised up out of the world and caught up into heaven, being assured that he loves her too well to let her remain at a distance from him always. She will sometimes go about from place to place singing sweetly; and seems to

be always full of joy and pleasure, and no one
knows for what. She loves to be alone, walking in the fields and groves and seems to have
some one invisible always conversing with
her." Mrs. Edwards proved a real helpmeet
to her husband and as his reputation spread
throughout the colony her name was always
associated with his. Of her an old writer says:
"She paid a becoming deference to her husband;
she spared no pains in conforming to his inclinations and rendering everything in the
family agreeable and pleasant, accounting it
her greatest glory, and that wherein she could
best serve God and her generation, to be the
means in this way of promoting his usefulness
and happiness. And no person of discern-
ment could be conversant in the family without observing and admiring the perfect harmony, the mutual love and esteem that
subsisted between them." In some ways the
world was not very kind to Edwards. There
were times when poverty and persecution
seemed to be his only reward. Believing as
he did, he could not help thinking that he
had fallen upon evil days. Yet we cannot
help feeling glad that for him the tragedy of
existence was relieved by a beautiful home
life and the presence of one able and willing
to help bear his burdens.

"In the church of the wilderness Edwards wrought,
Shaping his creed at the forge of thought;
And with Thor's own hammer welded and bent
The iron links of his argument,
Which strove to grasp in its mighty span
The purpose of God and the fate of man!
Yet faithful still in his daily round
To the weak and the poor and sin-sick found,
The schoolman's lore and the casuist art
Drew warmth and life from his fervent heart.
Had he not seen in the solitudes
Of his deep and dark Northampton woods
A vision of love about him fall?
Not the blinding splendor which fell on Saul,
But the tenderer glory that rests on them
Who walk in the New Jerusalem;
Where never the sun or moon are known
But the Lord and his love are the light alone!
And watching the sweet, still countenance
Of the wife of his bosom rapt in trance,
Had he not treasured each broken word
Of the mystical wonder seen and heard;
And loved the beautiful dreamer more
That thus to the desert of earth she bore
Clusters of Eshcol from Canaan's shore?"

Independently of his personal renown the ministry of Edwards in the beautiful old New England town of Northampton occupies an important place in the ecclesiastical history of New England on account of the mighty revival, known as "The Great Awakening," which visited the parish in 1741. It was in

this movement that the New England Calvinist was associated with Whitefield, the
golden-mouthed Chrysostom of the eighteenth
century. Much has been written in regard
to "The Great Awakening," particularly in
reference to the excesses which characterized it.
There is, however, ample evidence to prove
that all of the influences of this revival were
not negative. Beyond the peradventure of a
doubt it "revitalized the dying orthodoxy of
New England and turned the minds of many
from the things that are of the earth to the
eternal verities."

In some quarters nevertheless Edwards was
severely criticized for some of the methods which
he used during the great spiritual upheaval.
He was blamed for "frightening poor, innocent
little children with talk of hell-fire and damna-
tion." And no matter how sympathetic our
attitude, we must admit that some of his
writings lend color to such accusations. In
speaking of children he says, "They are young
vipers, and are infinitely more hateful than
vipers, and are in a most miserable condition
as well as grown persons; and they are naturally
very senseless and stupid, being born as the
wild ass's colt, and need much to awaken
them." This they doubtless got, for we have
ample evidence that the doctrine of fire-and-

brimstone was an important phase of Edwards's theology. Here it might not be amiss to quote from his best-known sermon, "Sinners in the Hands of an Angry God": "The God that holds you over the pit of hell, much as one holds a spider or some loathsome insect over the fire, abhors you and is dreadfully provoked; his wrath toward you burns like fire; he looks upon you as worthy of nothing else but to be cast into the fire; he is of purer eyes than to bear to have you in his sight; you are ten thousand times more abominable in his eyes than the most hateful venomous serpent is in ours. O sinner! consider the fearful danger you are in: it is a great furnace of wrath, a wide bottomless pit, full of fire of wrath that you are held over in the hand of that God, whose wrath is provoked and incensed as much against you as against many of the damned in hell. You hang by a slender thread with the flames of divine wrath flashing about it, and ready to singe it and burn it asunder." Recourse to the sermons of the shepherd of the Northampton flock show that at this period the people of that village were very frequently regaled with pabulum of this kind. We could possibly find here an explanation of some of the indisputable evils which followed "The Great Awakening."

But within a couple of years the village
resumed its ordinary tranquillity. Later, however, a bitter church war between priest and
people burst with almost unrestrained fury
upon the little parish. To-day the village of
Northampton is most heartily ashamed of its
ungenerous treatment of the most distinguished
man who ever dwelt within its borders. There
is something nevertheless to be said on their
side of the question. One of Edwards's admiring biographers speaks of him as "thorough
in the government of his children." Sir Leslie
Stephen says: "He adopted the plan, less
popular now than then, and even more de-
cayed in America than in England, of 'thor-
oughly subduing' his children as soon as they
showed any tendency to self-will. He was a
'great enemy' to all 'vain amusements,' and
even after his children had grown up he en-
forced their abstinence from such 'pernicious
practice' and never allowed them to be out
after nine at night. Any gentleman, we are
happy to add, was given proper opportunities
for courting his daughters after consulting
their parents, but on condition of conforming
strictly to the family regulations. This Puritan discipline appears to have succeeded with
Edwards's own family; but a gentleman with
'flacid solids, rapid fluids,' and a fervent be-

lief in hell-fire is seldom appreciated by the youth even of a Puritan village."[1]

Edwards brought charges against a number of prominent young people of his congregation, accusing them of reading improper literature, very probably Richardson's Pamela. These accusations, involving practically all of the prominent families in the community, set the town in a blaze. At the same time a more serious battle was being waged as to who was eligible for admission to the Lord's Supper. To enter at length at this time into the intricacies of a church quarrel in a New England village in the middle of the eighteenth century would not be particularly edifying. We shall content ourselves with chronicling the result. Edwards was dismissed from his parish by a majority of more than two hundred to twenty, "a martyr to his severe sense of discipline." Thus at the age of forty-seven he found himself, with no means and a large family, turned adrift. It takes the night to bring out the stars; it takes adversity to bring out the best that is in a man. In his hour of darkness the frail, persecuted preacher never looked back but boldly set out to make the best of things as they were. Friends came to his aid; there were several pulpits ready to

[1] Printed by permission of G. P. Putnam's Sons, Publishers.

accept his services; one call came from far-away Scotland. But for some inexplicable reason the position which he accepted was that of missionary to the Indians at Stockbridge, Massachusetts. There is something both of the comic and the tragic in the idea of the great Calvinistic logician attempting to teach the rudiments of Christianity to the copper-colored children of the sun. It is rather hard to decide though whom we most pity, Edwards or the Indians. Stephen says: "He has remarked pathetically in one of his writings on the very poor prospect open to the Houssatunnuck Indians, if their salvation depended on the study of the evidence of Christianity. And if Edwards preached upon the topics of which his mind was fullest, their case would have been still harder. A sermon in the Houssatunnuck language, if Edwards ever acquired that tongue, upon predestination, the differences between the Arminian and the Calvinist schemes, liberty of indifference, and other such doctrines, would hardly be an inproving performance."

Whatever its influence upon the lives of the Indians, Edwards's exile in the wilderness was an important period of his life. Here it was that he wrote his famous treatise upon the Freedom of the Will, which can be regarded

as one of the literary sensations of the century.
In regard to this essay there has been much
darkening of council by words without knowledge. Fulsome laudation and wholesale con-
demnation together have been its portion.
For a couple of generations it has been the
fashion to speak of it as a monumental work
with whose conclusion no one agrees, but
containing arguments which none can dispute.
A little analysis of the work itself, however,
conclusively proves that there is absolutely no
need of such a cowardly surrender to Calvinism. At the outset, even taking it for granted
that we could find no flaw in Edwards's
logic that would not prove the correctness of
his reasoning, it would simply be an evidence
of our unfortunate inadeptness at the dis-
covery of verbal chicanery. To unravel all of
the caustical intricacies of the essay on the
Will would simply be as profitable as the
solving of the puzzle in the old syllogism in
which David informs us that all men are liars.
Life is a little bit too big to be compressed
into a few pedantic syllogisms.

But there is no earthly reason for assuming
the technical correctness of the reasoning in
this marvelous analysis of the fundamental
doctrine of the Pilgrim Fathers. In short,
Edwards argues that everything has a cause,

that we select one thing rather than another
because we are influenced by our strongest
motive. The will, being determined by the
strongest motive, is not free. In speaking of
this argument Dr. Charles F. Richardson, of
Dartmouth, says: "Its practical value is nil.
Upon the thoughts, words, and deeds of life
it exerts no effect. Before one choose A or
B, it is true, he must make up his mind which
to choose; having chosen, perhaps he cannot
choose the other; at any rate, he cannot have
chosen other than he did choose. What
follows as to his real freedom of choice in the
first place? Practically nothing. Can a man,
before choosing, select A or B at will? Yes,
unless he is a puppet, and no subtlety or
nullification of words can make this other
than a fact. It was by a free act that Edwards
determined to write his treatise. Writing it
in Stockbridge, he could not also write it
elsewhere. And in spite of all its evident and
potent environment, the completed volume
was the work neither of chemical forces merely,
nor the Fates, nor of the pen of God."

Edwards tried to solve an unsolvable problem. Most of us are satisfied with the dictum
of bluff old Samuel Johnson, "We know we're
free and that's the end of it." Man's vision
is limited. He cannot see all sides of truth.

It is true that

> "There's a divinity that shapes our ends,
> Rough-hew them how we will";

but it is also true that

> "Our wills are ours, we know not how;
> Our wills are ours, to make them thine."

The essay on the Will is an attempt to achieve the impossible. We may wonder at the magnitude of the work. We may admire it for its dialectical skill, but at the best we cannot pronounce it other than a magnificent failure.

The fame which Edwards won through his *opus magnum* caused him to be appointed president of the College of New Jersey at Princeton. Upon this appointment Dr. Oliver Wendell Holmes in his brilliant but very unsympathetic essay makes the following comment: "The truth is, Edwards belonged in Scotland, to which he owed so much, and not to New England. And the best thing that could have happened, if it had happened early enough, both for him and for his people, was what did happen after a few years of residence at Stockbridge, where he went after leaving Northampton, namely, his transfer to the presidency of the College at Princeton, New

Jersey, where the Scotch theological thistle has always flourished, native or imported—a stately flower at present, with fewer prickles and livelier bloom than in the days of Boston, the Ettrick Shepherd of old." Whether he was capable of winning for himself a place by the side of Witherspoon, McCosh, Wilson, and the other great presidents of Princeton is a question upon which it is idle to speculate. Less than a month after taking up the duties of his office he died of smallpox and was buried in the little Presbyterian graveyard at Princeton by the side of his son-in-law and predecessor, Dr. Aaron Burr, in the same plot in which later was laid all that was mortal of another Aaron Burr, Edwards's grandson, who brought dishonor to an honored name.

The life of Edwards is full of contradictions. Genius is always a paradox. Attempts to analyze it are mostly futile. But the fact remains that Jonathan Edwards was great among the sons of men. His title among American thinkers will not soon be disputed. On a memorial tablet on the wall of the church of the parish from which he was once driven with excoriations we read these words: "The law of truth was in his mouth and iniquity was not found in his lips. He walked with me in peace and equity and did turn many away from iniquity." And he of whom the words can be truly said was one of the "friends and aiders of those who live the life of the Spirit."

III

RADIANT VIGOR

In his strong, vivid, and inspiring poem "Rugby Chapel," Matthew Arnold, in speaking of his father, Dr. Thomas Arnold, the great master of Rugby, says:

> "But cold,
> Solemn, unlighted, austere
> Through this gathering darkness, arise
> The chapel walls, in whose bound
> Thou, my father, art laid.
>
> "There thou dost lie, in the gloom
> Of the autumn evening; but ah!
> That word 'gloom' to my mind
> Brings thee back in the light
> Of thy radiant vigor again.
> In the gloom of November we passed
> Days not dark by thy side;
> Seasons impaired not the ray
> Of thy buoyant cheerfulness clear."

In the phrase "radiant vigor" we find epitomized the vital personality of the English schoolmaster, who to the youth of more than one generation was a veritable tower of strength, When Thomas Arnold became a candidate for the Headmastership of Rugby, it was pre-

dicted that if he were elected, "he would change
the face of education all through the public
schools of England." This he did not do
through any revolutionizing of the scholar-
ship of his day, but, rather, by the contagion
of a powerful personality. He had vigor of
body and vigor of soul. It must be admitted
that in general physical vigor is the basis of
all strength. A strong intellect is mostly
found in a strong body. Bodily health is
conducive to a genuine spirituality. It is
hard for a dyspeptic to be a saint. Samuel
Johnson once said in his blunt way, "Every
man is a rascal when he is sick." Seldom is
the radiant, life-giving personality found in
the tenement of clay of an invalid. No longer
do we believe "mortification of the flesh" to
be an act of piety.

> "Let us not always say,
> 'Spite of this flesh to-day
> I strove, made head, gained ground
> Upon the whole!'
> As the bird wings and sings
> Let us cry, 'All good things
> Are ours; nor soul helps flesh more now
> Than flesh helps soul.' "

The body is not to be looked upon as weight
impeding the growth of the soul but, rather,
as its helper and ally.

It cannot, however, be denied that in regard to the power of a strong body to in-
vigorate the spirit there has been within
recent years considerable empty verbalizing.
In some circles it is the fashion to quote
the hopelessly over-worked proverb, *"Mens
sano in corpore sano,"* as meaning that
the possession of a sound body is incontrovertible evidence of the presence of a
sound mind.   I once heard an address
upon what the speaker called "Muscular
Christianity." His title may have been correct, for what he called Christianity was most
emphatically neither intellectual nor spiritual.
Sometimes the much-vaunted triangle of "body,
mind, and spirit" is discussed in such a way
as to cause the listener to believe that the
first line of this hypothetical figure is of vastly
more importance that the other two. But in
spite of the callow vaporing of those who, in
the worst sense of the phrase, possess "single-
track" minds, health of body as a factor in
the development of the soul must not be
minimized.

"Radiant vigor" is the most potent force of
human dynamics. It is at the heart of all
real teaching. Almost everybody who writes
or speaks along educational lines has his own
definition of education. Is there, however,

any of these formulations which comes nearer to hitting the nail square on the head than Thomas Carlyle's scintillating apothegm, "Fire kindled at the fire of living fire"? Real teaching is from the living, through the living and to the living. No pedagogical course can make a teacher of a gerund-grinding depersonalized pedant. Neither can a theological seminary transform such an one into a real preacher of the living word. The radiantly vigorous personality is, after all, the outgrowth of a great soul. The man of lean soul has no power of inspiration. Among the great preachers of the last century, like a mountain in the clear, cold air of morning, towers the radiant figure of Phillips Brooks. A Japanese student at Harvard, after hearing him one Sunday morning in Trinity Church, wrote: "Phillips Brooks! What struggling souls does he support and strengthen! What a depth under his surplice, what a broadness behind his prayer book! After a draught of his elixir a wayfarer marches on for a week or two with songs upon his lips; the rough earth with all its mountains and valleys leveled before him." More than one choice youth has caught new gleams of the vision splendid as through Dr. Allen's biography he comes into sympathetic contact with this big-souled prophet of the invisible. No man stood nearer to the life of midnineteenth-century America than Henry Ward Beecher. Eloquent, magnanimous, open-minded, sympathetic, and sincere, he spoke not alone to the congregation of Plymouth Church but to the American people. The source of this Herculean power lay in a personality of radiant charm and vigor. As George William Curtis once said, "How few of us can keep our balance when a regal soul dashes by." Character is not taught but caught. Human betterment comes through association with the best. In gauging the worth of a life it can be truly said, "So much personality, so much power."

Little is there which a man can do without finding his personality a help or a hindrance. For example, nervous, sinewy English sentences are never written by nonentities. The carrying power of a group of words depends upon the man behind them. An assumed vigor of expression on the part of a weakling becomes a shriek. The red-blooded virility of Rudyard Kipling is the genuine expression of the man. The numerous pitiful imitations of this poet who, at his best, belongs among the masters are in themselves evidences of the futility of trying to acquire the art of writing by beginning at the wrong end. The development of the personality is the first step in the making of a writer. The blundering student who really says something which is the outgrowth of his own experience has greater potentialities than the prim miss who has acquired the ability to cover several pages with faultless nothings. Nowhere and never can we get away from what we are.

What an individual makes of himself is the final criterion of the success or failure of his life. In his somewhat raving soliloquy the youth in Tennyson's "Locksley Hall" curses among numerous other things "the gold that gilds the straighten'd forehead of the fool." Yet in the long run no amount of gilding can hide the real man. Education is not to be measured by the amount of knowledge accumulated but, rather, in terms of manhood and womanhood. It is not what we say or what we know or what we can do that counts, but what we are. One of the world's most comprehensive truths is expressed in the words, "As a man thinketh in his heart so is he." An individual's thoughts write themselves upon his very person. He who in thought grovels in the sensual mire becomes in his aspect coarse and animalistic. To concern oneself year after year with worthless trifles makes a man puttering and pedantic. The virtue of

economy practiced too faithfully becomes a
vice. Thinking in terms of pennies tends to
dwarf the mind and soul. Constant concern
with things material extirpates the power of
spiritual insight. Too dominant an emphasis
upon the financial aspects of religion unspir-
itualizes a church. The preacher who measures
success in terms of loaves and fishes becomes
a contemptible object. We have it on good
authority that there is no place for the money-
changer in the temple of Jehovah. Just as
true to-day as when they were first uttered
are the words of the wise man of old, "Keep
thy heart with all diligence, for out of it are
the issues of life." As we think, we are.

In H. G. Wells's Mr. Britling Sees It
Through we find an indirect tribute to Matthew Arnold when one of the characters de-
clares that England's troubles are due to the
fact that "we didn't listen to Matthew Arnold."
In the writings of this Victorian prophet of
"sweetness and light" there is at least one
thought that America needs. Arnold laid
special stress upon the ancient Hellenic ideal
of self-development, which teaches that the
highest due of man is to "augment the ex-
cellence of his nature and make an intelligent
being more intelligent." Some one may object, saying, "Is it not the duty of a Christian

to do good to others?" This question most
certainly deserves an affirmative answer, but
before we try to make others better and to
reform the world in general, it behooves us to
have ourselves attained a reasonable intellectual
and moral stature. The world cannot be re-
formed or evangelized by bunglers. Capacity
always comes before achievement. It is not
alone charity that begins at home. All progress starts with the individual. "But I am so
anxious to save souls," a young man said to
President Finney, of Oberlin, during an inter-
view in which the youth was trying to justify
his plan of entering the ministry without
completing his education. "Young man," said
the President, "if the Lord had wanted you to
go to saving souls a year sooner, he'd have
made you a year sooner."

Sometimes we spend so much time cultivating
our neighbor's gardens that weeds run riot in
our own. But in the words of Thoreau the need
is for men who are "not only good, but good
for something." Hours used in self-improve-
ment are sometimes spent in a more essentially
religious way than some that were passed in
distributing tracts. It was Matthew Arnold
himself who spoke of Sophocles as being one
who "saw life steadily and who saw it whole."
In the last analysis it is the strong, well-

balanced individual with this broad, clear
perspective who carries forward the banner of
humanity. Radiant vigor is a grace never
attained by those who see but one aspect of
truth. It does not fall as the gentle rain from
heaven upon the place beneath. Like all of
the other real attainments of life, it must be
paid for with wisdom, tolerance, restraint, and
effort. But it is worth the price.

The man who has this dynamic energizing
power is as strong as the strongest. He is a
real leader of the host of mankind. In the
same noble poem, inspired by his father's
life and character, the poet in winged words
lays his wreath of laurel upon the altar of
the captains in the army which fights the
battles of truth and light:

> "Then, in such hour of need
> Of your fainting, dispirited race,
> Ye, like angels, appear,
> Radiant with ardor divine!
> Beacons of hope, ye appear!
> Languor is not in your heart,
> Weakness is not in your word,
> Weariness not on your brow.
> Ye alight in our van! At your voice,
> Panic, despair, flee away.
> Ye move through the ranks, recall
> The stragglers, refresh the outworn,
> Praise, reinspire the brave!

Order, courage return.
Eyes kindling, and prayers,
Follow your steps as ye go.
Ye fill up the gaps in our files,
Strengthen the wavering line,
Stablish, continue our march,
On, on to the bound of the waste,
On, to the city of God."

IV

THE SPIRITUAL MESSAGE OF WHITTIER[1]

DURING the years in which Whittier lived and wrote, the hills and valleys of New England were resounding with the tumult and shouting of a long-waged ecclesiastical conflict. The old order was changing, yielding place to the new. The harsh, dogmatic, logical, positive Calvinism of an earlier day was inevitably reacting into a nebulous but militant Unitarianism. Young men in libraries were closing their Paleys and grappling with the intricacies of a Kantean transcendentalism. Still, to a large degree, unknown in Europe, the greatest book of the nineteenth century, Sartor Resartus, was in America finding readers among men of light and leading and the mighty message of the flaming-hearted, golden-mouthed prophet of Dumfries's purple moors was burning its way into the souls of men. From the lecture platform Emerson was giving to inquiring minds a somewhat misty and shallow

---

[1] The selections from Whittier are used by permission of Houghton Mifflin Company, Publishers.

philosophy, but a vital and luminous interpretation of life. The scintillating Dr. Holmes
with zest was tilting his shining lance against
the monstrosities of the old Calvinism. The
age was rife with subtle questionings. On
every side could be heard the clash of creed
and the babel of isms. Emerson said that the
motto of Margaret Fuller was: "I don't know
where I'm going. Follow me." And not a
few of her contemporaries could have sounded
the same slogan.

But in the religious poetry of Whittier we
are taken far away from the world of dogma
and controversy. His grasp of religious truth
is at once simple and comprehensive. His
message is essentially spiritual rather than
theological. The emphasis is upon the great
elemental, fundamental truths of the life of
the Spirit. Whittier's muse rises with wings
as eagle's above the smoke of the conflict.
The devotee of any creed can find solace and
refreshment at the Valclusa fountain of the
genius of the Quaker poet.

Whittier only among our great American
poets was not a Unitarian, although the
Unitarianism of Holmes and Longfellow was
the expression of a revulsion from the harsh
creed of their fathers rather than a denial of
the deity of the Christ. To claim that he was

a Unitarian is to ignore some of the sweetest
and noblest measures in our literature. But
the Christ whom he worshiped was not a dead
Christ upon whose grave the silent Syrian stars
look down. In the poem "Our Master" we
find words which upon the wings of song have
carried many a world-tossed, sin-burdened soul
to the throne of God:

> "No fable old, nor mythic lore,
>   Nor dream of bards and seers,
> No dead fact stranded on the shore
>   Of the oblivious years;
>
> "But warm, sweet, tender, even yet
>   A present help is He;
> And faith has still its Olivet,
>   And love its Galilee.
>
> "The healing of his seamless dress
>   Is by our beds of pain;
> We touch him in life's throng and press,
>   And we are whole again.
>
> "Through him the first fond prayers are said
>   Our lips of childhood frame,
> The last low whispers of our dead
>   Are burdened with his name.
>
> "We faintly hear, we dimly see,
>   In differing phrase we pray;
> But, dim or clear, we own in thee
>   The Light, the Truth, the Way!"

"The Meeting" is one of the great medi-
tative poems of our literature. It has the grand

old virtue of sincerity. Amid the perfumed brightness of the summer day in the plain little meetinghouse the farmer folk gather in silence to be still and know that God is God. And for them, towering above all others like a mountain in the clear, cold air of morning, looms one great truth:

> "... the dear Christ dwells not afar,
> The king of some remoter star.
> Listening, at times, with flattered ear
> To homage wrung from selfish fear,
> But here, amid the poor and blind,
> The bound and suffering of our kind,
> In works we do, in prayers we pray,
> Life of our life, he lives to-day."

Through all of the warp and woof of Whittier's poetry like a golden thread runs the sublime thought of the "living Christ," and nowhere is it more nobly expressed than in the ringing measures of "Palestine":

> "Blest land of Judæa! thrice hallowed of song,
> Where the holiest of memories pilgrimlike throng;
> In the shade of thy palms, by the shores of thy sea,
> On the hills of thy beauty, my heart is with thee.
> .   .   .   .

> "Blue sea of the hills! in my spirit I hear
> Thy waters, Gennesaret, chime on my ear;
> Where the Lowly and Just with the people sat down,
> And thy spray on the dust of his sandals was thrown.
> .   .   .   .

"And what if my feet may not tread where he stood,
　Nor my ears hear the dashing of Galilee's flood,
　Nor my eyes see the cross which he bowed him to bear,
　Nor my knees press Gethsemane's garden of prayer.

"Yet, Loved of the Father, thy Spirit is near
　To the meek, and the lowly, and penitent here;
　And the voice of thy love is the same even now
　As at Bethany's tomb or on Olivet's brow."

Theologically Whittier was neither a radical nor a reactionary. He was always anxious to conserve the precious heritage of other years, but the windows of his soul were ever open to new light and new truth. In the poetry of the gentle-spirited son of a sect which in earlier days the men of blood and iron of the old Puritan theocracy had excoriated and violently persecuted, we find no spirit of bitterness. In fact, in the verse of Whittier we find a tolerance for the Ironside Calvinist which is lacking in the works of their own descendants. He says,

"Hold fast your Puritan heritage,
　But let the free thought of the age
　Its light and hope and sweetness add
　To the stern faith the fathers had."

And again,

"Praise and thanks for an honest man,
　Glory to God for the Puritan!"

No man was more conscious than he that the Puritan, with all of his uncompromising harshness and his lack of sweetness and light, had a sense of the eternal values. Whittier understood this because he too endured as seeing Him who is invisible.

"Over the roofs of the pioneers
  Gathers the moss of a hundred years;
  On man and his works has passed the change
  Which needs must be in a century's range;
  The lands lie open and warm in the sun,
  Anvils clamor and millwheels run—
  Flocks on the hillsides, herds on the plain,
  The wilderness gladdened with fruit and grain!
  . . . .

"Everywhere is the grasping hand,
  And eager adding of land to land;
  And earth, which seemed to the fathers meant
  But as a pilgrim's wayside tent—
  A nightly shelter to fold away
  When the Lord should call at the break of day—
  Solid and steadfast seems to be,
  And Time has forgotten Eternity!

"But fresh and green from the rotting roots
  Of primal forests the young growth shoots;
  From the death of the old the new proceeds,
  And the life of truth from the rot of creeds;
  On the ladder of God, which upward leads,
  The steps of progress are human needs.
  For his judgments still are a mighty deep,
  And the eyes of his providence never sleep;
  When the night is darkest he gives the morn,
  When the famine is sorest the wine and corn!"

In those hours when we stand in the presence
of the mighty mysteries, when the lamp of
faith burns low and the specters of the mind,
like Banquo's gory ghost, refuse to down, the
simple and sincere faith of the New England
poet is a veritable rock in a weary land. Whittier reaches his affirmation not by following
the steep and rugged path of philosophical
questioning but, rather, by merely listening to
the promptings of the still small voice within
his own soul. The Quaker creed of the inner
light is but another phrasing of John Wesley's
grand old doctrine of the "witness of the
Spirit." But Whittier is not satisfied simply
to believe in the existence of God. Not only
has he faith in a God but in a good God. His
Deity is not the Calvinistic God of stern justice
and merciless wrath, but one who notes the
fall of every sparrow and who, "though the
road be dark and dreary," leads his children

"O'er moor and fen, o'er crag and torrent, till
The night is gone."

The poem "The Eternal Goodness" more nearly
than any other synthesizes Whittier's creed:

"Yet, in the maddening maze of things,
    And tossed by flood,
To one fixed trust my spirit clings:
    I know that God is good!

·   ·   ·   ·   ·   ·   ·   ·

"The wrong that pains my soul below
  I dare not throne above,
I know not of his hate—I know
  His goodness and his love.

. . . .

"I know not what the future hath
  Of marvel or surprise,
Assured alone that life and death
  His mercy underlies.

. . . .

"And so beside the Silent Sea
  I wait the muffled oar;
No harm from him can come to me
  On ocean or on shore.

"I know not where his islands lift
  Their fronded palms in air;
I only know I cannot drift
  Beyond his love and care."

But Whittier was no futile nurse of pious emotions. He never tried to substitute feeling for faith or faith for works. He understood that emotion not translated into deeds is baneful and that faith without works is dead. The man who sacrificed his best years to battling for the consummation of a great reform had translated his theology into human terms.

"To Thee our full humanity,
  Its joys and pains, belong;
The wrong of man to man on thee
  Inflicts a deeper wrong.

"Who hates, hates thee, who loves becomes
  Therein to thee allied."

His love for his fellow man was not a mere
wishy-washy sentimentality. With Carlyle he
believed, "When thou seest ignorance, animality, and brute-mindedness, smite it in
God's name." Strong and steady were the
blows which he struck the institution of human slavery. Paradoxical as it may seem,
the Quaker poet was the most militant of our
American writers. There are times when his
words ring as the trumpet summoning to the
fray.

> "... in God's own might
> We gird us for the coming fight,
> And strong in him whose cause is ours
> In conflict with unholy powers,
> We grasp the weapons he has given—
> The Light and Truth and Love of Heaven."

Not one of the sturdy virtues of the Puritan was lacking in the Quaker, but in him
there was a milder strain. He had a deeper
sense of brotherhood and a broader spirit of
tolerance. His religion was not so exclusively
dominated by Old Testament ideals. Love as
well as righteousness was in his lexicon, yet
he was ever loyal to duty. This characteristic
of his peculiar people is with translucent clearness mirrored forth in the poetry of Whittier.
In the cycle, "The Tent on the Beach," one
of the poems tells the story of "Abraham

Davenport." It was on the famous dark
day in May in 1780. The sky was so black
with ominous clouds that the birds ceased to
sing, the barnyard fowls went to roost, and
the cattle lowed at the pasture bars and looked
homeward. All expected to hear the doom-
blast of the trumpet shatter the heavy sky.
In the old State House sat the lawmakers of
Connecticut. Some one said, "It is the Lord's
great day," and moved adjournment.

> "... and then, as if with one accord,
> All eyes were turned to Abraham Davenport.
> He rose, slow cleaving with his steady voice
> The intolerable hush. 'This well may be
> The Day of Judgment which the world awaits;
> But be it so or not, I only know
> My present duty, and my Lord's command
> To occupy till he come. So at the post
> Where he hath set me in his providence,
> I choose, for one, to meet him face to face—
> No faithless servant frightened from my task,
> But ready when the Lord of the harvest calls;
> And therefore, with all reverence, I would say,
> Let God do his work, we will see to ours.
> Bring in the candles.' And they brought them in.

> "And there he stands in memory to this day,
> Erect, self-poised, a rugged face, half seen
> Against the background of unnatural dark,
> A witness to the ages as they pass,
> That simple duty hath no place for fear."

In an almost forgotten little poem, "The Friend's Burial," we find a precious tribute to the memory of one of whom it could be said as of the woman who broke the alabaster box of ointment at the Master's feet, "She hath done what she could."

> "How reverent in our midst she stood,
>   Or knelt in grateful praise!
> What grace of Christian womanhood
>   Was in her household ways!
>
> "For still her holy living meant
>   No duty left undone;
> The heavenly and the human blent
>   Their kindred loves in one.
> . . . .
> "The dear Lord's best interpreters
>   Are humble human souls;
> The Gospel of a life like hers
>   Is more than books or scrolls.
>
> "From scheme and creed the light goes out,
>   The saintly fact survives;
> The blessed Master none can doubt
>   Revealed in holy lives."

"Philosophy," says Novalis, "bakes no bread, but gives us God, freedom, and immortality." The real poet too brings to the soul of man a more vivid consciousness of the reality of the invisible. In Whittier we sound not the depth of struggling souls, we find no burning desire to

> ". . . assert Eternal Providence
> And justify the ways of God to men,"

neither do we view as in a magic mirror the varied life of a great age. But we do come face to face with the never-dying truths which the "ripening experience of life" taught a dauntless and loving soul; one whose sincere and genuine humanity draws him humanly near to our hearts. To sneer at Whittier because he has not the almost all-inclusive message of a Shakespeare or the superabundant vigor of a Browning is to give a pitiable example of that sophomoric sciolism which believes that those ideas that are easily comprehensible are invariably superficial. Obscurity and profundity are not necessarily synonymous terms; neither is simplicity an incontrovertible evidence of shallowness. Whittier's poetic assurances of immortality are of infinitely more worth than many labored volumes.

His thoughts here are those of a man who over doubt has gloriously triumphed. "My Psalm" is a poem which expresses the unwavering faith of life's eventide:

> "I mourn no more my vanished years:
>   Beneath a tender rain,
> An April rain of smiles and tears,
>   My heart is young again.

·   ·   ·   ·   ·   ·   ·   ·

"Enough that blessings undeserved
　　Have marked my erring track;
That wheresoe'er my feet have swerved,
　　His chastening turned me back;

"That more and more a Providence
　　Of love is understood,
Making the springs of time and sense
　　Sweet with eternal good;

"That death seems but a covered way
　　Which opens into light,
Wherein no blinded child can stray
　　Beyond the Father's sight;
　　.　.　.　.　.　.　.　.
"And so the shadows fall apart,
　　And so the west-winds play;
And all the windows of my heart
　　I open to the day."

But the poem of Whittier which is nearer
and dearer to our hearts than any other is
"Snowbound." Its Flemish pictures of old
days can never fade from memory's wall.
Without the icy breath of winter blows o'er
the land while around the great fireplace sits
the household in tumultuous privacy of storm
and

"... the old, rude-furnished room
Burst flower-like into rosy bloom,"

a bloom which will ever glow upon the pages
of our American literature. In how many and
many a life does "Snowbound" strike an an-

swering chord! As the poet's words ring in our hearts, fond memory throws the light of other days around us. We sit again by hearth-fires that have long grown cold and dream of those whom here we see no more and long

> "... for the touch of a vanished hand
> And the sound of a voice that is still."

Like Tennyson's "In Memoriam," "Snow-bound" is a cluster of blossoms from the valley and the shadow of death. It was written at an hour of loneliness and darkness and at least one of its stanzas came from an aching heart. Of his sister he writes thus:

> "As one who held herself a part
>   Of all she saw, and let her heart
>   Against the household bosom lean,
>   Upon the motly-braided mat
>   Our youngest and our dearest sat,
>   Lifting her large, sweet, asking eyes,
>   Now bathed in the unfading green
>   And holy peace of Paradise.
>   Oh, looking from some heavenly hill,
>   Or from the shade of saintly palms,
>   Or silver reach of river calms,
>   Do those large eyes behold me still?
>   With me one little year ago:
>   The chill weight of the winter snow
>   For months upon her grave has lain;
>
> .   .   .   .

The birds are glad; the brier-rose fills
The air with sweetness; all the hills
Stretch green to June's unclouded sky;
But still I wait with ear and eye
For something gone which should be nigh,
A loss in all familiar things,
In flower that blooms, and bird that sings.
And yet, dear heart! remembering thee,
  Am I not richer than of old?
Safe in thy immortality,
    What change can reach the wealth I hold?
    What chance can mar the pearl and gold
Thy love hath left in trust with me?
And while in Life's late afternoon,
    Where cool and long the shadows grow,
I walk to meet the night that soon
    Shall shape and shadow overflow,
I cannot feel that thou art far,
Since near at need the angels are;
And when the sunset gates unbar,
    Shall I not see thee waiting stand,
And, white against the evening star,
    The welcome of thy beckoning hand?"

But another stanza of "Snowbound" marks the high-tide of Whittier's poetry:

"What matter how the night behaved?
What matter how the north-wind raved?
Blow high, blow low, not all its snow
Could quench our hearth-fire's ruddy glow.
O Time and Change! with hair as gray
As was my sire's that winter day,
How strange it seems, with so much gone
Of life and love, to still live on!

Ah, brother! only I and thou
Are left of all that circle now—
The dear home faces whereupon
That fitful firelight paled and shone.
Henceforward, listen as we will,
The voices of that hearth are still;
Look where we may, the wide earth o'er,
Those lighted faces smile no more.
We tread the paths their feet have worn,
    We sit beneath their orchard trees,
    We hear like them the hum of bees
And rustle of the bladed corn;
We turn the pages that they read,
    Their written words we linger o'er,
But in the sun they cast no shade,
No voice is heard, no sign is made,
    No step is on the conscious floor!
Yet Love will dream, and Faith will trust
(Since He who knows our need is just),
That somehow, somewhere, meet we must.
Alas for him who never sees
The stars shine through his cypress-trees!
Who, hopeless, lays his dead away,
Nor looks to see the breaking day
Across the mournful marbles play!
Who hath not learned, in hours of faith,
    The truth to flesh and sense unknown,
That Life is ever lord of Death,
    And Love can never lose its own!"

Words like these the world will not willingly let die.

Whittier's deep and tranquil spirituality not only finds expression in his distinctively re-

ligious poetry, but it passes beyond this and
pervades more or less fully the whole body
of his work. In it there is no Calvinistic gloom
and severity but peace, light, love, and child-
like trust. In the religious poetry of the New
England Quaker we find a mingling of Puritan
and Friend, of Justice and Love, of the stern
creed of the dauntless Genevan and the simple
faith of leather-clad George Fox. It was
John Robinson, the pastor in Leyden of the
men and women of the Mayflower, who uttered
the pregnant sentence, "There is more light
and more truth in God's blessed Word than
has yet been revealed." The great gulf that
is fixed between the dogmatic horrors of Michael
Wigglesworth's "Day of Doom," the typical
poem of the old New England, and the win-
some inclusiveness of the simple creed of the
Quaker poet demonstrates the significant fact
that for two centuries of American life the
thoughts of man had been widening with the
process of the suns. The bells from a thousand
steeples had rung out the darkness of the
dismal days of The Scarlet Letter and the
Salem witchcraft. In the poetry of Whittier
we live in the brighter light of a nobler day.
And as we walk over the mountains and
through the valleys of life we can stand more
firmly and fight better because our souls have

been refreshed as we tarried with this sweet-voiced, clean-souled poet by the fountains of life abundant.

Although there are still among us those who remember the poets of the New England renaissance as they came and went among their fellows, it was more than a quarter of a century ago that the last of that shining company passed to where beyond these voices there is peace. Emerson, the serene earthquake scholar of Concord, and Longfellow, the gentle singer of our national springtime, died in the early eighties. Lowell, the youngest of the group, born over a century ago, February 22, 1819, died in the old elm-shaded home of his boyhood in 1891. A year later ended the tranquil life of the militant, serene hermit of Amesbury. In 1894 the lambent soul of the genial old autocrat, "the last leaf on the tree," felt the gentle touch of the breath of an eternal morning. To-day our souls thrill with the mighty impulses of a tremendous age. New voices are in the air and eyes that once were holden are seeing new visions. But not all that has come to us from other generations should be allowed to gather mold among the forgotten archives of the past. The writer who deals with the fundamentals of life and of character has eternal youth. From the

quiet cottage at Amesbury have come lines
heard around the world. Generations yet un-
born will through the words of John Greenleaf Whittier learn the truths of God. Though
dead he yet speaketh.

> "There is no end for souls like his;
> No night for children of the day."

V

THE ART OF BEING HUMAN

ONCE when Father Taylor was lying upon what was supposed to be his deathbed, some one said, "Well, Father, you'll soon be with the angels." Quick as a flash the old preacher replied: "I don't want angels. I want folks." After all, human sympathy is the quality which more than any other draws us to its possessor. We cannot help liking the person who has it. In some parts of the United States there is a provincialism which expresses an idea for which orthodox terminology is lacking. It is customary to speak commendatorily of a person as common. This is almost another word for human. Happy is he who meets the "common" man or woman. He whose experiences have given him human sympathy has that which is worth more to the world than the most minute and abstruse knowledge gathered in classroom and libraries.

Dean Shaler once said, "I have known many an ignorant sailor or backwoodsman who, because he has been brought into sympathetic contact with the primitive qualities of his

kind, was humanely a better educated man
than those who pride themselves on their
culture." The French have a proverb, which
being translated says, "Born a man and died
a grocer." With slight emendations this
epigram can be adapted to dehumanized individuals in various fields of activity: "Born a
man, and died a broker." Or it may be "and
died a preacher" or "a college professor."
The Germanization of the American university
during the decades following the Franco-
Prussian war has tended to produce the narrow
specialist and the seed-pecking critic. Limi-
tation of interests tends to shrivel the soul.
The story is told of a lady who met at a dinner
a well-dressed, attractive man with whom she
unsuccessfully tried to carry on a conversa-
tion. Among the subjects which she intro-
duced were politics, literature, music, and even
people, but she could get not a gleam of re-
sponse. Finally, with consummate social tact
the gentleman himself came to her rescue by
saying, "I can't talk about these things. My
line is lumber." A man's life is just about as
large as the range of his interests. Nothing
will take the place of the vital touch with
things human. William James was able to
make psychology thrill with life because he
himself was vitally human. Professor Louns-

bury made the ordinarily sleep-producing subject of philology glow with genuine interest
because he personally was in touch with the
real things of earth.

For over a quarter of a century William
Dean Howells was the unchallenged dean of
American letters. Seventy-odd volumes came
from his tireless pen. Not one of them is the
product of any fantastic feat of the imagination. He simply chronicled the life which he
sympathetically observed. From the banks of
the Ohio to romance-haloed Venice was a long
journey. But to this kindly, tolerant, brotherly
lover of books and men, life was always life.
To read the memory-gilded pages upon which
he has written of a Boy's Town, along the great
river whose changing and haunting beauty
has not been lost although it no longer flows
through a pathless wilderness as it did in the
days when the birch bark canoe of the red
man ruffled its gleaming waters, is vicariously
to live the life of truth-loving, warm-hearted
men and women of the days that are no more.
As in the Years of My Youth we come into
contact with the ideas and ideals of a later
boyhood home not far from the sea-green
waves of Lake Erie we feel the thrill of the
westward march of the Puritan spirit. The
man who depicted the subtle charm of Brahman

New England, the hypnotic fascination of the seething whirl of our American Babylons, the inimitable charm of England's gray-stone abbeys and ivy-clad towers, found no dull pages in the world's varied volume. In the following sentence Howells epitomizes the source of his own attractive power: "The way to be universally interesting is to be universally interested."

The world to-day is every whit as interesting as it was when Chaucer's pilgrims journeyed from the Tabard Inn in Southwark to Canterbury. "Books," says Stevenson, "are a mighty bloodless substitute for life." We read so that we can better understand the real world which is mirrored forth in the world of letters. Without attempting to add to the high plethora of definitions of education, it can be truly said that education means the broadening of an individual's experience. President Thwing tells us that most college men who fail in life do so because of an inability to get along with people. A man can succeed in no public capacity unless he understands humanity. He cannot do this unless he has previously known intimately and appreciatively dozens, possibly hundreds, of people in both literature and life.

The late Dr. William T. Harris, for many years commissioner of education, once spoke of literature as "vicarious experience." What a world of suggestion in the phrase! The man whose knowledge of life depends upon his own personal experience is almost certain to be "cabined, cribbed, confined" in his outlook upon the world's thought and activities. Real literature is not something to give to "airy nothing a local habitation and a name." Writing that is not irradiated with life is sounding brass and tinkling cymbal. Shakespeare looms great among the children of genius because his range of human sympathy was larger than that of any other man who has recorded the thoughts of his heart upon the printed page. George Eliot has written volumes characterized by an encyclopedic learning, but the books which for generations to come will keep her memory green are those which tell of the men and women whom she learned to know and love in her girlhood among the hedgerows of Warwickshire. The best of Emerson comes not from his "transcendental moonshine," but from his power to see below the surface in the lives of flesh and blood men and women. Being quoted a million times will not make threadbare Pope's truth, "The proper study of mankind is man."

To value books more than people means arrant pedantry. To treat persons as though

they are things is a cardinal sin against society.   Broadmindedness, some widely · pro-
claimed opinions to the contrary notwithstand-
ing, does not necessarily mean laxity of ethics.
Neither is the person with definite ideas in
regard to right and wrong invariably narrow
in his outlook. The broad man is one of broad
sympathies and wide affinities. His most dis-
tinguishing characteristic is the power to put
himself in another person's place. He can
disagree with his neighbor and at the same
time respect him and his point of view. The
old deacon who said, "If I am wrong, I am
willing to be convinced, but I'd like to see
the man who could do it," merely furnished
a most delightful illustration of the intoler-
ance of crass stupidity. The really humanized
son of Adam does not want to make the world
over after his own pattern.

The surest way for an individual to de-
personalize himself is to make his life a namby-
pamby imitation of the career of some one
else.   Emerson says in his essay on "Self-
Reliance," "We come to wear one cut of face
and figure and acquire by degrees the gentlest
asinine expression." The man who goes with
the crowd will never be anything but one
of them. A subservient follower never makes a
leader. He who is too cowardly to live his

own life annihilates his personality. Insipidity
is the reward of the imitator. No one can do
our living for us. We must make our own
decisions and abide by their consequences.
No decision in the last analysis is a wrong
decision. In regard to the larger issues of life
it is impossible to long halt between two
opinions. "He that is not for me is against
me." To live a life of half-hearted negative-
ness or of cowardly compromise means the
subtle but certain deterioration of the very
foundations of the soul. Weakness breeds
weakness: strength begets strength. Power of
decision means ruggedness of personality.

Snobbishness is another impeder of the
development of a sincere, attractive personality. In the Standard Dictionary we read the
following: "Snob—a vulgar pretender to gen-
tility or superior position; one who regards
wealth and position rather than character."
In other words, a snob is one who cares more
for appearance than reality; one who substitutes false standards for those that are
true. For him life is not real; it is merely a
spectacle. His world is a stage upon which
he can "strut and fret." He does not enjoy
good society but takes pleasure in being seen
in it. It was said of a certain ecclesiastical
politician in England that he was "a dexterous

worshiper of the rising sun." In his lexicon a
friend was one who could advance his interests.
But, after all, the world is so constructed that
it pays a man to be his real self and to judge
other human beings by the genuine standards
of worth.

A number of years ago an American politician
won considerable notoriety by coining the
proverb, "A cheap coat makes a cheap man."
Was there ever more falsity compressed into
seven words? Many a man worth his weight
in gold has worn a cheap coat. Abraham
Lincoln with his homemade shirt and "jeans"
trousers, upheld by one "yarn gallus" and
terminating somewhere between the knees and
the ankles was not a "cheap man." In real
worth of manhood there was enough of him
to outweigh at least a thousand of the perfumed poodles of the gold coast. A number of
years ago I noticed a great crowd standing
in the corridor of a metropolitan railroad sta-
tion. Upon inquiring the cause of the gather-
ing I discovered that a certain widely adver-
tised wife-hunting, fortune-seeking duke would
pass that way in a few minutes. Soon the
eager, anxious throng was rewarded by the
sight of the son of a line of British earls, a
bandy-legged weakling with receding forehead
and evil, dissipated face. But his title won

for him an American wife and an American fortune. It is a tragically false measure of judgment which would make us bow before a title or wealth possessed by one with nothing else to commend him.

Equally obnoxious is the intellectual snob. Now and then we meet a man who goes through life with the assumption that because his name is on the alumni roll of some great institution he is among the chosen ones of earth, independent of his knowledge, his efficiency, his personality, or his character. If any of us acquire the habit of looking upon the education which we have been given at the expense of society as a possession which gives us the right to look with sneering contempt upon our fellow men, we become what Roosevelt called "undesirable citizens." "No man ever had a point of pride that was not injurious to him." To use a wrong criterion in judging either others or ourselves tends to corrode our lives and our souls with falseness.

It is, nevertheless, possible to be entirely sincere and unselfish without being human. In Wordsworth's little poem "She Was a Phantom of Delight" one of the finest tributes paid to his wife is in the line, "A creature not too bright or good for human nature's daily food." An outstanding fault in Tennyson's

"Idylls of the King" is his portrait of King
Arthur as a monstrosity of icy perfection.
Ice water in the veins is a poor substitute for
red blood. There are unfortunately attractive
sinners and sour saints. A human iceberg is
always a poor sort of a Christian. Oftentimes
a thin-lipped, critical, unsympathetic church-
man makes religion repulsive to an entire
community. Jesus did not glorify the narrow,
repressed, circumscribed life; he preached the
gospel of the life abundant. Long-facedness is
not a sign of spirituality. In the words of
Carlyle: "The man who cannot laugh is not
only fit for treasons, stratagems, and spoils,
but his whole life is already a treason and a
stratagem." The lack of a sense of humor
means the lack of imagination, and hard indeed is it for him afflicted in this way to have
a sympathetic understanding of life and of
humanity. But life itself is the greatest of
all teachers. We educate each other. The
better we know our fellow men the more tolerant we become. The years teach us that man
is not black spotted white, but white spotted
black. Experience is the real humanizer.

It is said that at a certain stage in the
initiation of the Buddhist priest the postulant
reaches a certain door and before he can pro-
ceed farther he is asked the question, "Art

thou a man?" "Art thou human?" is not an inappropriate interrogation with which to greet a young man standing at the portals of those professions which have to do not with things but with people. "What you are speaks so loudly that I cannot hear what you say." In the long run, success or failure depends upon what we make of ourselves. The elusive factor called personality is the most potent force beneath the shining stars. Man is his own ancestor. Edwin M. Stanton is quoted as saying: "Every man over fifty is responsible for his face." More than this we are the molders of our characters, the makers of our personalities. Arnold of Rugby was bigger than anything he did. In the biography of Mark Twain we find a man greater than the books which came from his pen. Andrew Carnegie was more than his millions. Roosevelt the man looms larger than Roosevelt the statesman. Thomas Carlyle as a Scotch farmer would have been a man of mark in his little world. There can easily be too many bloodless automatons of efficiency or depersonalized bundles of erudition, but never too many red-blooded, true-hearted, life-loving friends and helpers of mankind.

VI

THE WHITE WATER LILY

In Theodore Storm's modest little classic
Immensee, a book which epitomizes the tragedy
of a vanished hope, the young man walks in
the pale calm moonlight by the shores of a
tranquil inland sea. Before his eyes fair pictures come and go. He sees

> "Such sights as youthful poets dream
> On summer eve by haunted stream."

Far out upon the crystal surface of the fair
and placid lake like a fallen star there gleams
a solitary water lily, white as the clouds that
float beneath the blue sky of a summer's day.
An indescribable longing to possess the lonely
flower seizes the young man's heart. Soon
the sturdy strokes of the swimmer break the
stillness of the silent night. He swims and
swims, but still the lily is far, far in the dim
distance. At last he turns his face shoreward
and never once does he look back upon the
fragrant bloom which he had so ardently longed
to make his own. To this young man the
white flower symbolized one whom he had

loved and lost in the days when his sky was
gilded with the auroral light of youthful ro-
mance and his heart sang the dulcet strains
of love's old sweet song. But to strive for the
unattainable is the common lot of man.

We all live in two worlds. We know full
well this practical, everyday world, this world
of getting and spending, where the fittest
survive and the weak go down in the fight,
where the blight of sin and ignorance causes
the fairest flowers of life to fade and wither.
It is this realm of which Shelley sings in words
of real pathos:

> "We look before and after,
>   And pine for what is not;
> Our sincerest laughter
>   With some pain is fraught.
> Our sweetest songs are those
>   That tell of saddest thought."

But we live, too, in another world: in the
world of dreams: in the heaven-illumined land
of the ideal. Here we forget the harsher
realities of life and catch faint adumbrations of
the golden days which are yet to be. Here
there

> "... falls not hail or rain or any snow,
> Nor ever wind blows loudly; but it lies
> Deep-meadowed, happy, fair, with orchard lawns
> And bowery hollows crowned with summer sea."

For many of us the land ideal looms up against the misty backgrounds of the past. There is that within man which makes him idealize bygone days. The remembrance of them brings to the heart that

> ". . . feeling of sadness and longing
> That is not akin to pain,
> And resembles sorrow only
> As the mist resembles the rain."

It is this feeling of sadness which the deep-voiced Tennyson describes in words of never-dying melody:

> "Tears, idle tears, I know not what they mean.
> Tears from the depth of some divine despair
> Rise in the heart, and gather to the eyes,
> In looking on the happy autumn fields,
> And thinking of the days that are no more."

We stand upon the summit of the mountain and view the road by which we have ascended as it winds through the valley and over the foothills and our souls are thrilled by its beauty. We see it curve through sylvan dells, through fertile farms, through the tree-embowered village. We forget the long and toilsome journey, the blazing sun of the noonday, the summer storms that blew from the mountains. Across the emerald-clad sward of the years, like the sound of sweet bells in tune, come the words of New England's crystal-toned bard:

"I can see the breezy dome of groves,
  The shadows of Deering's Woods
And the friendships old and the early loves
Come back with a Sabbath sound, as of doves
  In quiet neighborhoods.
And the verse of that sweet old song,
It flutters and murmurs still:
'A boy's will is the wind's will,
And the thoughts of youth are long, long thoughts.'

"I remember the gleams and the glooms that dart
  Across the schoolboy's brain;
The song and the silence in the heart,
That in part are prophecies and in part
  Are longings wild and vain.
And the voice of that fitful song
Sings on, and is never still:
'A boy's will is the wind's will,
And the thoughts of youth are long, long thoughts.'

"Strange to me now are the forms I meet
  When I visit the dear old town,
But the native air is pure and sweet,
And the trees that o'ershadow each well-known street,
  As they balance up and down,
Are singing the beautiful song,
Are sighing and whispering still:
'A boy's will is the wind's will,
And the thoughts of youth are long, long thoughts.' "

When fond memory throws the light of other days around us we live amid the Arcadian beauty of the land ideal.

But life's golden age is never in the past. Dreams of a brighter future make it easier for men to bear the burdens of a darkened present. The lank, ungainly backwoods boy, who lay before the open in a rude Illinois cabin reading over and over Mason Weems's quaint old Life of Washington, forgot the poverty and crudeness of his surroundings as he looked across the future's untrodden fields to the day when on his shoulders would rest the mantle of the Cincinnatus of the West. The boy who trod the towpaths of the Western Reserve dreamed of the thousands whom he should some day sway by the power of his eloquence.

On a rocky New England farm, so lonely that even now ever and anon the white-footed deer forsakes his leafy covert and drinks from the streamlet in the meadow, there lived and toiled a dark-eyed Quaker lad. How hard was his lot! How narrow his life! But Greenleaf Whittier had seen the vision. The plowboy of the Merrimac valley had heard the lutelike voice of the plowman of the bonnie fields of Ayr. The light that never was on land or sea shone over that barren little farm and the world is richer to-day because that Quaker lad followed the gleam.

Long ago, when the spacious times of the great Elizabeth were fading in sweeping clouds of glory from the earth, the youthful John Milton set before himself the sublime ideal of writing a poem which the world would not willingly let die. Even then did he realize that he who would write an heroic poem must first live an heroic life. He passed through the fiery furnace of young manhood without the smell of smoke upon his garments. Year after year he burned the scholar's lamp of toil and sacrifice. When the clouds of fratricidal war hung like a pall over the land he doffed his singer's mantle blue and donned the armor of an intellectual gladiator. In the battle for the liberty of the English people the quiet scholar stood in the foremost ranks. Sorrow walked with him. The day came when the blind bard sat in ever-enduring darkness and saw no more

> "The sweet approach of even or morn,
>   Or sight of vernal bloom or summer's rose,
>   Or flocks, or herds or human face divine."

The men who with him battled in the halls of state and those as well who upon the field of carnage had fought for Cromwell and the

Lord were wandering fugitives and outcasts in
distant lands or daily laying down their lives
upon the crimson scaffold; where once the rugged, stern, indomitable old Oliver had bowed
before the throne of the Lord God of Israel a
licentious, lascivious, voluptuous court con-
temned all that was pure and righteous and
holy. In that hour of darkness and peril and
gloom John Milton gave to the world a poem
that it will never let die. When the time
came for him to pass to where beyond these
voices there is peace his dying lips were heard
to murmur, "Still guides the heavenly vision."

"Where there is no vision the people perish."
It is the vision splendid which impels men to
forsake the primrose path of ease and walk
the rough and stony road of usefulness, a
road which many, many times has been the
path by which the sons of earth have reached
the tablelands above.

> "Not once or twice in our fair island-story
> The path of duty was the way to glory.
> He that, ever following her commands,
> On with toil of heart and knees and hands,
> Through the long gorge to the far light has won
> His path upward and prevailed,
> Shall find the toppling crags of Duty scaled
> Are close upon the shining tablelands
> To which our God himself is moon and sun."

He who follows the vision climbs the steep
ascent through peril, toil, and pain. Wendell
Phillips was a ten-talented man; fortune had
emptied her horn at his feet. He was what
Dr. Holmes called "A Brahman of the Brahmans." In his veins flowed New England's
bluest blood; physical beauty and mental
capacity alike were his portion; to him the
sirens of ambition sang their sweetest songs;
the world stretched before him full of pleasant
possibilities. Already he saw himself the
idol of society, the spokesman of New England conservatism in the halls of the nation,
the successor of the golden-mouthed Webster,
the compatriot of the idolized Sumner. But,
like the note of a battle trumpet a call re-
sounded throughout the length and breadth
of the land, and when the young lawyer heard
it, it did not fall on unresponsive ears. Then
he felt, as he afterward said, "I love inex-
pressibly these streets of Boston over which
my mother led my baby feet; and if God grants
me time enough, I shall make them too pure
for the footsteps of a slave." In the years to
come, in every great struggle against long-
entrenched evil, his was the white plume that
ever waved in the forefront of the embattled
hosts of righteousness. Uncompromising, in-
tolerant, and profoundly mistaken as he some-

times was, the world is a better place because
this New England idealist lived in it. The
time will come when his eloquence, "like the
song of Orpheus, will fade from a living memory
into a doubtful tale," but two thousand years
hence the echoes of his regal soul will not be
silent; the memory of his dauntless courage,
his heroic sacrifice, and his unswerving loyalty
to truth shall not have perished from the
earth.

The ideal ever molds the man. "He who
surrenders himself to a great ideal becomes
great." Long ago it was written, "As a man
thinketh in his heart so is he." Lowell says:

> "Of all the myriad moods of mind
>   That through the soul come thronging,
> Which one was e'er so dear, so kind,
>   So beautiful as Longing?
> The thing we long for, that we are
>   For one transcendent moment,
> Before the Present poor and bare
>   Can make its sneering comment."

The man whose ideal is the heroic becomes a
hero. The youth who in the realm of the
vision lives in contact with greatness becomes
great. They who think of those things which
are true and honest and just and pure and
lovely and of good report grow in grace and

in beauty of personality as the years go by.
The vision splendid may fade into the
light of common day, but it leaves a glory
behind it.

Yet the youth who swam out across the
lake for the white water lily came back without it. Many of the noblest of earth's ideals
have never been realized. Often when we
seize the flower its bloom is shed. Sometimes
when we think of the world's multitudinous
incongruities we feel that life is a succession
of comedies. Then we can sympathize with
the words of Thackeray: "Such people as
there are living and flourishing in the world—
faithless, hopeless, and charityless. Let us
have at them, dear friends, with might and
main." But when we look deeper, more and
more we feel that life is a tragedy more real
than any depicted by the pen of an Æschylus
or Shakespeare. In this tragi-comedy of life
seldom is it that man reaches the goal of his
aspirations. Whittier's familiar folk-ballad,
"Maud Muller," strikes an answering chord
in many a heart:

> "God pity them both! And pity us all,
> Who vainly the dreams of youth recall.

> "For of all sad words of tongue or pen,
> The saddest are these: 'It might have been!'

"Ah well! for us all some sweet hope lies
  Deeply buried from human eyes;

"And, in the hereafter, angels may
  Roll the stone from its grave away!"

In every life there is some sad sweet "might
have been." There is a faded hope and an
unrealized ideal.

"Something beautiful has vanished,
  And we sigh for it in vain,
  And we seek it everywhere,
  On the earth and in the air,
  But it never comes again."

Yet often the vanished ideal is the supreme
glory of a life. In an address delivered at
Harvard College one of America's most eminent
and high-minded statesmen said: "Ideals are
like stars. They are not to be reached but to
be followed."

I remember in my boyhood hearing the old
men talk about the underground railway
days when the rural calm of my native valley
was broken by the advent of the Southern
slave drivers, with their iron fetters and their
baying hounds, in search of their runaway
property. Often have I been shown the lonely
road by which these pursued and timorous
black men stole by night from the valley to
the hospitable farmhouse among the blue hills

to the north. Many a time on snowy moonlight nights as I traveled that road I thought
of the dusky pilgrims from the sloping banks
of the rivers of Old Virginia and the cotton-
whitened fields of Dixie's southernmost lands.
Often I saw above me, as my thoughts turned
to those who had once trodden that winding
highway, the north star which those wanderers followed so many weary miles amid the
thick darkness of night, shining pure, steady,
and serene just as it shone on untold generations of those whom here we see no more.
They who followed that star never reached it,
but they reached the freedom for which they
longed. To them it was the beacon which
led to liberty. A man's ideal is his polar star;
he may never attain it, but by following it
he may reach the higher altitudes and the
purer atmosphere of a better country, a land
where life is larger and fuller and richer and
freer. It is not the accomplishment which
counts but the honest effort. One of the most
deep-sighted seers who ever walked the shores
of earth once told us:

"Not on the vulgar mass
　Called 'work' must sentence pass,
　Things done that took the eye and had the price;
　O'er which, from level stand,
　The low world laid its hand,
　Found straightway to its mind, could value in a trice:

"But all the world's coarse thumb
And finger failed to plumb.
So passed in making up the main account,
All instincts immature,
All purposes ensure,
That weighed not as his work, yet swelled the man's
    amount;

"Thoughts hardly to be packed
Into a narrow act,
Fancies that broke through language and escaped,
All I could never be,
All men ignored in me,
That was I worth to God, whose wheel the pitcher
    shaped."

The fight for the ideal may be a losing fight, but it is never a fight in vain. Phillips Brooks says, "If you aim at the stars you will hit the tree tops." Man is better for every high ideal, for every noble purpose, for every lofty aspiration. There have been idealists who have worn the laurel wreath of victory; there have been those who have sadly trodden the *via dolorosa* of affliction and defeat, but the God who notes the fall of every sparrow, who hath clothed the lilies of the fields with ineffable fragrance and beauty, knoweth them all by name, and, like the stars, they shall shine in his firmament forever and ever. But the real idealist is not the idle dreamer of any empty day who sails away from the lands of

earth on ethereal seas of abstractions.   He
understands that

> "The common problem, yours, mine, everyone's
> Is not to fancy what were fair in life
> Provided it could be—but, finding first
> What may be, then find how to make it fair
> Up to our means: a very different thing."

In the never-dying words of Tennyson we
read of that glorious company who gathered
around the blameless Arthur's throne: of the
pure Sir Percival; of Gareth in all the splendor
of his youthful beauty; of Launcelot, the
bravest and the strongest of the knights; of
Galahad, with the strength of ten because his
heart was pure.   Upon a later, sadder, darker
day we hear the once proud king tell of how
he made them lay their hands in his and
swear

> "To reverence the King, as if he were
> Their conscience, and their conscience as their King.
> To break the heathen and uphold the Christ,
> To ride abroad redressing human wrongs,
> To speak no slander, no, nor listen to it,
> To honor his own word as if his God's,
> To lead sweet lives in purest chastity,
> To love one maiden only, cleave to her,
> And worship her by years of noble deeds,
> Until they won her

.   .   .   .

Not only to keep down the base in man,
But teach high thought, and amiable words
And courtliness, and the desire of fame,
And love of truth and all that makes a man."

But there fell before the lances of these brave
and valiant knights the robber barons who
preyed upon the poor. One by one their
proud castles yielded. No more was the long
howling of the wolves to be heard amid the
snow. Peace smiled again upon the land.
The wilderness and the solitary place were
made glad and the desert blossomed as the
rose. Chivalrous knights worshiped at the
shrine of fair and gracious womanhood. A
wise and good ruler in many-towered Camelot
meted out even-handed justice to all who
bowed before his throne. But there came a
time when war, famine, and desolation once
more cast their shadow over Arthur's realm,
when a renegade knighthood and a faithless
queen brought sorrow to the heart of the
blameless ruler, when in his anguish he sadly
cried, "My knights have followed wandering
fires and left present wrongs to right themselves." Sad is it indeed when life-detached
ideals call men away from the common duties of
common life to follow a glimmering light which
leads to nowhere; nevertheless the world cannot but pay its meed of praise, of well-deserved

praise, to the unswerving tenacity, the dauntless daring, and the heroic spirit of self-sacrifice
which very often is the portion of the follower
of the wandering fire. But lofty idealism without practical efficiency is of little avail. The
efficient idealist is no melancholy, mild-eyed
lotus eater, who muses and dreams and
broods with half-shut eyes while the great
currents of life sweep irresistibly by. Yet it
is "In deeds he takes delight." All of life
is not included in the "practical." As the
hart panteth after the water brooks the spirit
of man longs to rise, with wings as eagles,
above the things of time and place. No life
is so dark that it cannot be illumined by the
presence of the heaven-born ideal; no heart
is so despondent that it cannot pulsate with
hope. The white water lily very often sheds
its fragrance upon lonely moor and desolate
fen. "We are such stuff as dreams are made
on." Man can never live by bread alone.
He must endure as seeing Him who is invisible.

VII

THE FUNDAMENTAL TEACHING OF THOMAS CARLYLE[1]

WHEN Thomas Carlyle gave his inaugural address as Lord Rector of the University of Edinburgh, memory threw around him the light of other days and he lived once more in that year of the long ago when he left the hills of Dumfriesshire for the ancient seat of learning in whose halls he once more stood. "It is now," he said, "fifty-six years gone last November since I first entered your city, a boy of not quite fourteen, to attend the classes here, and gain knowledge of all kinds, I could little guess what, my poor mind full of wonder and awe-struck expectation." Unlike his American friend, Emerson, Carlyle did not spring from a line of scholars. He was the first of his race to grapple with the mysteries of books. His boyhood home was a peasant's cottage, and the greatest lessons of his life were those which he learned by its fireside. His strong,

---

[1] By permission of The Methodist Review, Nashville, Tennessee.

sturdy, earnest, veracious father and his gentle, affectionate, yearning, solicitous mother were both fundamentally religious. Their religious heritage was Dissent. They belonged to the group known as "Burgher-Seceders," or "New Lichts." Their son tells us that "a man who awoke to the belief that he actually had a soul to be saved or lost was apt to be found among the dissenting people." The most tenderly cherished ambition of the Carlyles for their nobly endowed first-born son was that some day he should "wag his pow in the pulpit." It was to prepare him to be a spiritual leader that they toiled and sacrificed in order to send him to the university.

But, as has been true of many another father and mother, the hopes of James and Janet Carlyle were not to be realized in the way which they expected. In those years at Edinburgh the young student was called upon to battle with "spiritual dragons." In his life there came hours when he felt that the old faith, hallowed by the sweetest and most precious memories, was naught but the idle dream of a darkened age. It also became more and more apparent that a dyspeptic genius like Thomas Carlyle would by no means be an ideal pastor for any people. He was called upon to endure years of doubt and drifting. But as the years passed one by one the clouds vanished from his sky.

It was in June, 1821, when he was twenty-six years of age, when, as he says, he "authentically took the devil by the nose" and began to attain those convictions by which his later life was governed. In 1830, in speaking of this period of liberation, he says, "This year I found that I had conquered all my skepticisms, agonizing doubts, fearful wrestlings with the foul, vile, and soul-murdering mud-gods of my epoch; had escaped from Tartarus, with all its Phlegetons and Stygian quagmires, and was emerging free in spirit into an eternal blue of ether where, blessed be heaven, I have, for the spiritual part, ever since lived, looking down upon the welterings of my poor fellow-creatures in such multitudes and millions still stuck in the fatal elements, and have no concern whatever in their Puseyisms, ritualisms, metaphysical controversies, and cobwebberies. I understood well what the old Christian people meant by conversion—by God's infinite mercy to them. I had in effect gained an immense victory, and for a number of years, in spite of nerves and chagrins, had a constant inward happiness that was quite royal and supreme, in which temporal evil was transient and insignificant, and which essentially remains with my soul, though far oftener eclipsed and lying deeper down than then. Once more thank heaven for its highest gift."

The doubts which so long like a fog had surrounded him had departed. In the battle with fear faith was triumphant. It could be said of him as Tennyson wrote of Arthur Hallam:

"He fought his doubts and gathered strength,
    He would not make the judgment blind,
    He faced the specters of the mind
And laid them; thus he came at length

"To find a stronger faith his own,
    And power was with him in the night,
    Which makes the darkness and the light,
And dwells not in the light alone."

From that time forth in many a noble volume, some of which the world will not willingly let die, Thomas Carlyle preached a gospel, which with "true prophetic eloquence" has reached the hearts of men. No man has spoken to our modern times with more of the spirit and power of the stern, militant, truth-loving, truth-telling prophets of Israel. Over against the cynical doubt of the skeptic, Carlyle set the "Everlasting Yea" of the great God. He was a heaven-sent messenger proclaiming the law of truth, the nobility of labor, the glory of independence and the dominance of the "eternal verities." He was a preacher of repentance, of righteousness, and of retribution. He was perhaps the most potent ethical and religious force of his century. And to-day, when most of the shovel-hatted, mammon-worshiping ecclesiastics of his generation have gone their journey to a lasting oblivion, the voice of the rugged, titanic old Scotchman is still lifted against wrong and still sounds a message of inspiration and of hope.

Carlyle's theology, like the man himself, is a bundle of paradoxes. To attempt to unravel its intricate threads would mean the facing of a task of almost terrifying formidableness. The author of Sartor Resartus and The French Revolution exercised to the utmost the prerogative of genius to be inconsistent. But at least a word may be said in regard to the great writer's fundamental creed. Most emphatically he was not, as has been inanely said, "a great thinker without a theology." No man can do real thinking in regard to the vaster issues of life and entirely ignore theology. Professor Nichol in his life of Carlyle, after attempting to find Carlyle's creed by the process of elimination, writes the following pregnant paragraph: "What, then, is left of Carlyle's creed? Logically little, emo-

tionally much. If it must be defined, it is
that of a Theist with a difference. A spirit
of flame from the empyrean, he found no
food in the cold Deism of the eighteenth century. He inherited and determined to persist
in the belief that there was a personal God—a
Maker, voiceless, formless." To Emerson he
writes in 1836, "My belief in a special Providence grows yearly stronger, unsubduable,
impregnable"; and later he said, "Some strange
belief in Providence was always with me at
intervals." Thus while asserting that "all
manner of pulpits are as good as broken and
abolished," he clings to the old Ecclefechan
days.

"To the last," says Mr. Froude, "he believed
as strongly as ever a Hebrew prophet did in
spiritual religion." He recommended prayer as
"A turning of one's soul to the highest."
Many times he spoke confidently of his belief
that when a man dies he shall live again. On
the death of Mrs. Carlyle's mother he wrote
to her: "We shall yet go to her. God is great,
God is good." But later this confident assurance seems to have been replaced by a calm,
uncertain hope.

Intellectually Carlyle had journeyed far from
the faith of the Burgher-Seceders of his native
village, but to the end of his life he was essen-

tially Puritan. He tried to tear away the
husks and keep the kernel. He was not, however, entirely successful in doing this. Carlyle
would have been a happier man, and in some
respects a better man, if his life had been
dominated by the vital Christianity of a
Robert Browning. He excoriated Unitarians,
but intellectually had much in common with
them. Certain essentials of Christianity he
threw away as "Hebrew old clothes." It is
equally true that Carlyle was never able to
completely rid himself of "the old clothes"
of Calvinism. All of his life he did his thinking more in terms of the Old Testament than
of the New. Herein lay his strength and his
weakness. He has been plausibly called "A
Calvinist tinctured with German idealism."
The Kantean transcendentalism with which
Carlyle's wide reading had brought him into
contact had to some extent opened the windows of his mind. He had naturally discarded
some of the monstrosities of the crude Puri-
tanism of his early environment. But the
metaphysic of Calvinism was the most potent
influence of his life.

It is by turning from Carlyle's ill digested,
haphazard theology to his militant, glowing,
and sincere philosophy of life that we find
the source of his Herculean strength. Even

though clouds and darkness at times surrounded him for over half a century, he preached to upward-striving, light-seeking men and women the gospel of the reality of the spiritual. He called his generation to turn from the meat which perisheth to the eternal verities. To him as to any spiritually minded man, the idea of an absentee God and a mechanical universe was chilling and repulsive. The thought of God and of his presence in the world inspired some of Carlyle's most magnificent lines. In the chapter of Sartor Resartus entitled "The Everlasting Yea" we read: "Fore-shadows, call them rather fore-splendors of that Truth and Beginning of Truths, fell mysteriously over my soul. Sweeter than Dayspring to the shipwrecked in Nova Zembla; ah, like the mother's voice to her little child that strays bewildered, weeping, in unknown tumults; like soft streamings of celestial music to my too-exasperated heart, came that Evangel. The Universe is not dead and demoniacal, a charnelhouse with specters; but Godlike and my Father's!"

To an age of preeminent scientific achievement he said: "With our Sciences and our Cyclopedias, we are apt to forget the divineness in these laboratories of ours. We ought not to forget it. That once well forgotten, I

know not what else were worth remembering.
Most sciences, I think, were then a very dead
thing; withered, contentious, empty—a thistle
in late autumn. These sciences without this
are but the dead timber; it is not the growing
tree and forest—which gives ever-new timber,
among other things. Man cannot know either
unless he can worship in some way."

In Carlyle's day materialism as a philosophy
had its able and aggressive defenders. To-day
there is none so poor as to do it reverence.
But that which counts is not so much what
a man says he believes, or thinks he believes,
but that which he really believes with sufficient
intensity to translate into life. Wendell Phillips
once scathingly said that if an American saw
a silver dollar on the other side of hell he
would jump in for it. In his excellent volume
Personal Religion and the Social Awakening
Professor Ross Finney says: "The philosophy
of human life that dominates our own age,
permeates its atmosphere, and obsesses the
thought of nearly all our people is essentially
materialistic. We are convinced that a man's
life consists in the abundance of the things
which he possesses." We seek for evidences
of material success and power because they
constitute the measure of value in modern
life. Even in professions which exist primarily

to disseminate ideals there exists practically
the same standard of values. The trail of
the serpent is everywhere. Never was there
a more vital need of men keeping before them
the inclusive truth that the fundamental values
of life are not material but spiritual. In Heroes
and Hero-Worship Carlyle said, "A man's
religion is the great fact in regard to his life."
And with all of his dim gropings and thunderous sophistries for over half a century to
England and to mankind in fiery words of
golden eloquence he preached the Pauline
gospel: "To be spiritually minded is life, and
to be carnally minded is death."

Not only against mammonism did he lift
his mighty sword, but with the same fierce
energy and titanic power he battled against
the vapid dilettantism which sees in life nothing
but a primrose path of pleasure. There came
a time when he clearly saw that blessedness
lies not in receiving but in giving, not in
enjoying but in doing. The thought of the
sacredness of work loomed large in the
Carlylean philosophy of life. In Past and
Present we read: "All true work is sacred;
in all true work, were it but hand-labor, there
is something of divineness. Labor, wide as
the Earth, has its summit in Heaven. Sweat
of the brow; and from that up to sweat of the

brain, sweat of the heart, which includes all
Kepler calculations, Newton meditations, all
Martyrdoms—up to that 'agony of bloody
sweat' which all men have called divine.
O brother, if this is not 'worship' the more the
pity for worship, for this is the noblest thing
yet discovered under God's sky. Who art
thou that complainest of thy life of toil?
Complain not. Look up, my wearied brother;
see thy fellow workmen there, in God's eter-
nity." Against the "clay-given mandate,
'EAT THOU AND BE FILLED,'" he placed the
"God-given mandate, 'WORK THOU IN WELL-
DOING.'"

The idea of work cannot be dissociated from
duty. Carlyle's Calvinistic ethics was by no
means entirely negative in his life. He was
indoctrinated with the old Puritan idea of
righteousness. This inevitably meant an unswerving loyalty to duty. This son of the
ironside Scottish Calvinists believed not merely
in work but in work well done. As he looked
at the strong stone walls built by his father,
James Carlyle, master mason of Ecclefechan,
he said, "Let me write my books the way he
built his houses." "The best way," he says,
"to prepare for the great duties of life is to
do well the small duty." Carlyle's teaching
did not consist of a conglomerate of life-de-

tached theories; he was eminently practical. In one of his noblest passages he says: "The latest gospel in this world is, Know thy work and do it. Know thyself: long enough has that poor 'self' of thine tormented thee; thou wilt never get to 'know' it, I believe. Think it not thy business, this knowing of thyself; thou art an unknowable individual: know what thou canst work at, and work at it like a Hercules."

And again he says: "It has been written, 'an endless significance lies in work'; a man perfects himself by working. Foul jungles are cleared away, fair seed-fields rise instead, and stately cities; and withal the man himself first ceases to be a jungle and foul unwholesome desert thereby. Consider how, even in the meanest sorts of labor, the whole soul of man is composed into a kind of real harmony the instant he sets himself to work. Doubt, Desire, Sorrow, Remorse, Indignation, Despair itself—all these like Hell dogs lie beleaguering the soul of the poor dayworker as of every man: but he bends himself with free valor against his task, and all these are stilled, all these shrink murmuring far into their caves. The man is now a man. The blessed glow of Labor is in him; is it not as a purifying fire, wherein all poison is burnt up, and of sour smoke itself there is made a bright blessed flame?"

Carlyle understood that "happiness to be got must be forgot." The ripening experience of life taught him that if a man made it the object of his life to seek happiness, he was predooming himself to an existence of empty futility. He almost incessantly emphasized the fact that life is no mere "May-game for men." To his friend Sterling he said, "Woe unto them that are at ease in Zion." In Sartor Resartus he reiterates, "Love not pleasure, love God." To him as to the old Hebrews with whom he had so much in common, life was terribly and tragically earnest. With another great Puritan Carlyle believed that throughout his years upon earth he must live "As ever in his great Taskmaster's eye."

The old Calvinistic emphasis upon retribution was also one of the doctrines which he did not discard as a relic of mediæval barbarism. The fact of sin loomed large in his thinking. There are to-day those who by means of widely disseminated teachings, miscalled ethical, are permeating American life with the baneful falsehood that there is no clear distinction between right and wrong. To Carlyle right and wrong were considerably more than "ancient, outworn, Puritanic traditions." Ezekiel's awful truth, "The soul that sinneth, it shall die" was of mighty import in his theology.

In his Edinburgh address, in speaking to the students of his time-honored Alma Mater he said: "If you will believe me, you who are young, yours is the golden season of life. As you have heard it called, so it verily is the seedtime of life; in which if you do sow tares instead of wheat, you cannot expect to reap well afterward." "Platitudes" some would call such words. They certainly contain no new thought. Paul, in his letter to the Galatians, used the same comparison to express the same thought, "Whatsoever a man soweth that shall he also reap." Yet no greater truth ever came from the heart and mind of man. He who has learned it to do it has mastered the greatest lesson of life. Carlyle never wrote a line in conflict with this fundamental ethical law. He never, as did Goethe in Faust, depicted life in such a way as to give his reader the impression that a man could sin with impunity. It must be admitted that in his inexcusable whitewashing of that incarnation of blood and murder known as Frederick the Great he attempts to gloss over some of the most nefarious deeds ever perpetrated by human beings. But taking Carlyle's writings in mass they show that he loved right and hated

wrong with all the intensity of his Puritan
father.

His description of the deathbed of Louis XV
is in itself a sermon on "the exceeding sin-
fulness of sin." "Yes, poor Louis, Death has
found thee. No palace walls or lifeguards,
gorgeous tapestries or gilt buckram of stiffest
ceremonial could keep him out; but he is
here, here at thy very life-breath and will
extinguish it. . . . Unhappy man, there as thou
turnest, in dull agony, on thy bed of weariness,
what a thought is thine! Purgatory and Hell-
fire, now as all too possible in the prospect;
in the retrospect, alas, what thing didst thou
do that were not better undone; . . . what
sorrow hadst thou mercy on? Do the 'five
hundred thousand' ghosts who sank shame-
fully on so many battlefields from Rossbach
to Quebec, that thy Harlot might take revenge
for an epigram—crowd round thee in this
hour? Thy foul Harem; the curses of mothers,
the tears and infamy of daughters? Miserable
man! thou 'hast done evil as thou couldst':
thy whole existence seems one hideous abortion
and mistake of Nature; the use and meaning
of thee not yet known. Wert thou a fabulous
Griffin *devouring* the works of men; daily
dragging virgins to thy cave; clad also in
scales that no spear would pierce: no spear

but Death's? A Griffin not fabulous but real!
Frightful, O Louis, seem these moments for
thee.— We will pry no further into the horrors of a sinner's deathbed."

Carlyle's ethics was not a mass of abstract
philosophical theorems. It was rooted and
grounded in reality. He understood the in-
separable relation existing between conduct and
life. His fundamental ethical viewpoint can
best be expressed in the words of Emerson,
"The specific stripes may follow late after the
offense, but they follow because they accom-
pany it. Crime and punishment grow out of
one stem. Punishment is a fruit that, unsus-
pected, ripens within the flower of the pleasure
which concealed it." It was Carlyle himself
who said that Napoleon's empire was doomed
to destruction because it was founded on injustice. The Scottish Puritan, like Goethe,
his exceedingly unpuritanic teacher, knew full
well that although "the mills of God grind
slowly, they grind exceeding small." Some
have said that he taught that might makes
right. This, however, is almost diametrically
opposite to his teaching. Instead he believed
that right makes might. He knew that the
wages of sin is death, and this ancient and
universal truth of life he unflinchingly faced.

Taking it all in all, however, it was Carlyle's

social teachings which had the greatest influence upon the life and thought of his own
and succeeding generations. Carlyle would
have been a mighty force for social betterment had he done nothing more than inspire
John Ruskin to devote his life to righting deep-
intrenched wrongs. But it cannot be denied
that books like Chartism and Past and Present
were potent weapons in the battle for the
industrial and social liberation of the English
people. Nowhere is the human problem of
those early days better stated than in these
words: "England is full of wealth, of multifarious produce, supply for human want of
every kind; yet England is dying of inanition.
With unabated bounty the land of England
blooms and grows; waving with yellow harvests; thick-studded with workshops, industrial
implements, with fifteen millions of workers
understood to be the strongest, the cunningest,
and the willingest our earth ever had; these
men are here; the work they have done, the
fruit they have realized is here, abundant,
exuberant on every hand of us: and behold
some baleful fiat as of enchantment has gone
forth, saying, 'Touch it not, ye workers, ye
master-workers, ye master-idlers; none of
you can touch it, no man of you shall be the
better for it; this is enchanted fruit!' On

the poor workers such a fiat falls first, in its
rudest shape; neither can the rich master-
idlers, nor any richest or highest man escape,
but all are alike to be brought low with it,
and made poor in the money sense or a far
fataler one." His description in Past and
Present of the paupers in the workhouse of
St. Ives is one which it is not easy to forget.
Economics he excoriated as the "dismal science"; sociology was then in its dim begin-
nings; but he could readily see that where
there was starving in the midst of plenty,
poverty surrounded by luxury, sordid bru-
tality side by side with swinish epicureanism
there was a need of plain words and purpose-
ful action.

The years between 1830 and 1850, the period
in which was accomplished Carlyle's most
distinctive work, were marked by a political,
industrial, and social revolution of tremendous
moment. The people were beginning to make
themselves heard. The dominant classes were
compelled to relinquish a few of the privileges
which an unjust caste system had given them.
In 1828 the Test Act discriminating against
Protestant Dissenters was repealed. The next
year the Catholics won their victory in the
passage of the Catholic Emancipation Bill.
The First Reform Bill after a strenuous fight

was passed in 1832. This bill was essentially a victory for the bourgeoisie in their battle with the rural landowning class. To the laborer it meant little, but it was a step in the right direction. During the next decade considerable legislation protecting the rank and file of the people from economic and social injustice was placed upon the statute books of the realm. The great event of the early years of the reign of Victoria was the Anti-Corn Law movement led by Richard Cobden and John Bright. All over England men, women, and children were on the verge of starvation on account of the high tariff laws which had been passed to conserve the privileges of the landowning, game-preserving, lawmaking aristocracy. The fight was long and bitter, but June 25, 1846, the Corn Laws were repealed. Later came the agitation for a people's charter, giving the people of England still greater governmental prerogatives. This movement, which expressed the noblest idealism of many lives and contended for nothing more than simple justice, was not especially fortunate in its leadership and directly accomplished but little. Those were thrilling days in which to live. And Carlyle was not unawake to what was taking place around him.

He spoke of Peel's abolition of the Corn Laws as "the greatest veracity ever done." His interpretation of the deeper significance of chartism is both sympathetic and luminous. To many a young soldier in the army of the common good his words were both inspired and inspiring. The solution of the social problems by means of a benevolent despotism, such as he delineates in Past and Present, is of course palpably impossible. But no man of his generation had more at heart the ills of fellow men than Thomas Carlyle. And no man more lucidly and sincerely presented their cause. Some of his words sound surprisingly modern as we read them to-day. But in his demanding of economic justice he never failed to remember the fundamental reality of the spiritual. Here are words not without a high significance in the social gospel of Carlyle: "Brother, thou art a man, I think; thou art not a mere building Beaver or a two-legged Cotton-spider; thou hast verily a soul in thee, asphyxied or otherwise! Sooty Manchester, it is too built on the infinite Abysses; over-spanned by the skyey Firmaments; and there is birth in it, and death in it; and it is every whit as wonderful, as fearful, as unimaginable as the oldest Salem or Prophetic City. Go or stand, in what time, in what place we

will, are there not immensities, Eternities
over us, around us, in us."

Carlyle's passion for social justice, unlike
that of some modern intellectual amateurs, was
not an evanescent fad. It sprang from his
ingrained interest in humanity. Like Ben
Adhem he loved his fellow men. In Carlyle's
letters as found in the biography by Froude
there are many comments upon human beings
which give to the reader the impression that
Carlyle was anything but a lover of his kind.
It would be futile to deny that the sage of
Chelsea was very much in the habit of throwing showers of vitriol on all men and things.
Both he and his gifted wife were adept in the
art of making verbal etchings of the individuals whom they met from time to time.
And we are told that in etching use is made
of acids. Neither of the Carlyles was frugal
of acidic comment. His description of Rogers
is only too typical: "A most sorrowful, dis-
tressing, distracted old phenomena, hovering
over the rim of deep eternities with nothing
but light babble, fatuity, vanity, and the
frostiest London wit in mouth." One does not
have to read many pages of Carlyle's letters
in order to collect a few dozen acrimonious
personalities. But too much stress must not
be laid on these acerbities. He liked to talk,

and some of his characterizations read much more cruelly than they sounded. Moreover, it would not be at all difficult to chronicle example after example of deeds of sacrificing kindness on the part of the sharp-tongued Scotchman. In his last years the larger part of his income was consumed by his deeds of charity. He has written certain passages which for their sheer humanity are unsurpassed in the literature of any people.

In Sartor Resartus he says: "Poor wandering, wayward man! Art thou not tried, and beaten with stripes, even as I am? Ever, whether thou bear the royal mantle or the beggars gabardine, art thou not so weary, so heavy laden; and thy Bed of Rest is but a Grave. O my Brother, my Brother, why cannot I shelter thee in my bosom, and wipe away all tears from thy eyes?" Such words are not written by stony-hearted cynics. Another passage which could have been suggested by Millet's "Man With the Hoe" reads: "Pity him too the Hard-handed, with bony brow, rudely combed hair, eyes looking out as in labor, in difficulty and uncertainty; Rude mouth, the lips coarse, loose, as in hard toil and lifelong fatigue they have got the habit of hanging—hast thou seen aught more touching than the rude intelligence, so cramped,

yet energetic, unsubduable, true, which looks
out of that marred visage? Alas, and his poor
wife with her own hands, washed that cotton
neckcloth for him, buttoned that coarse shirt,
sent him forth creditably trimmed as she
could." Here there is anything but the callous
vapidity which sees in the toiling thousands
naught but crude material for cruder ridicule.

One of Carlyle's most beautiful and heart-
thrilling paragraphs is his tribute to his mother:
"Your poor Tom long out of his school days
has fallen very tired and lame and broken on
this pilgrimage of his, and you cannot help
him or cheer him any more; but still from your
grave in Ecclefechan churchyard you bid him
trust in God. That he will try if he can understand and do." According to his own theory,
he had found the secret of knowledge. In
understanding the man and his writings this
passage is considerable help: "One grand, in-
valuable secret there is, however, which includes all the rest, and, what is comfortable,
lies clearly in every man's power: To have an
open, loving heart, and what follows from the
possession of such. Truly it has been said,
emphatically in these days ought to be re-
peated, a loving Heart is the beginning of all
Knowledge." Carlyle may not always have
kept his heart open to new light and truth,

but in it always there dwelt the spirit of love.

In his old age Carlyle himself stated that he regarded truth as the Alpha and Omega of his message. Many an impetuous charge did he make against the citadels of falsehood. With him simple honesty was the crowning virtue. In speaking of his books he says: "I've had but one thing to say from beginning to end of them, and that was, that there's no other reliance for this world or any other but just Truth, and that if men did not want to be damned to all eternity they had best give up lying and all kinds of falsehood. That the world was far gone already through lying, and that there's no hope for it but just so far as men find out and believe the Truth and match their lives to it. But on the whole, the world has gone on lying worse than ever." In all of his writings, especially in Heroes and Hero Worship, do we see that his ultimate criterion in judging men is sincerity. He tells that Samuel Johnson, both practically and theoretically, preached this great gospel: " 'Clear your mind of Cant!' Have no trade with Cant: stand on the cold mud in the frosty weather, but let it be in your own real torn shoes."

It goes without saying that the generation

of Carlyle, just as much as that of Johnson,
needed to be exhorted to avoid cant and to
stand on the adamantine basis of reality. Is
there one who would contend that such teaching is entirely inapplicable to us of a later age?
In our speech how easy it is with superficial
fluency parrotlike to rehash the ideas and
words of others. Every profession has its own
particular brand of cant. There is no movement of the age which does not inspire the
eloquence of the retailer of second-hand verbi-
age. It is easy to substitute oracular piety
and long-faced religiosity for doing justice,
loving mercy, and walking humbly with God.
Nothing worth attaining is ever won without
a Herculean effort. Strength of character does
not fall as the gentle rain from heaven. Sincerity is the corner stone of real probity, but
it cannot be acquired except by those who
struggle to obtain it. Old-fashioned honesty,
unswerving loyalty to truth, and incorruptible
integrity are qualities which cannot loom too
large in any life. Sometimes the hardest task
which confronts an individual is to be honest
with himself. It takes more than mere verbal
sincerity to enable a man to look the facts
of life straight in the face. To acquire the
habit in the name of a silly optimism of glossing
over the disagreeable phases of existence

means, in the last analysis, the selling of one's
soul to the demons of falsehood. And it is
certain that the man who has given days and
nights to the study of the writings of Thomas
Carlyle will find it at least a little harder to
deviate from the straight and narrow path of
truth.

In Carlyle's passionate desire for reality we
find the key to his theory of history and of
life. Early in his career he set forth the idea
that the fundamental task of the writer is to
perceive and set forth the inexhaustible mean-
ings of reality. He believed, moreover, that
every fact, no matter how significant it might
appear, had latent within it some truth of
mighty import and that, above all else, man
is called to be loyal to fact. Right living to
him meant seeing the truth, proclaiming it,
and doing it. In the marvelous pages of his
essay on "Biography" he says: "Sweep away
utterly all frothiness and falsehood from your
heart; struggle unweariedly to acquire what is
possible in every God-created man, a free,
open, humble soul; speak not at all, in any
wise, till you have somewhat to speak; care
not for the reward of your speaking; then be
placed in what section of Time and Space
soever, do but open your eyes, and they shall
actually see, and bring you real knowledge,

wondrous and worthy of belief." In the
same article he gives expression to another
thought which cannot but have the ring of
inspiration to every man who labors for human
betterment: "Can we change but one single
soap-lather and mountebank Juggler into a
true Thinker and Doer, who even tries honestly
to think and do, great will be our reward."

This is what Carlyle for more than half a
century tried to do. And many a man of
light and leading has found his greatest teacher
in the sharp-tongued, rugged old Scotchman,
and upon the pages which he wrote has come
into contact with "truths that perish never."
Augustine Birrell, one of the cleverest of contemporary critics, has been quoted as saying,
"Young man, do not be in too great a hurry
to leave your Carlyle unread." In spite of
his angularities of personality and his profound errors of judgment, it cannot be denied
that few indeed are the men of modern times
who have meant as much to England and
mankind as this Chelsea "Isaiah of the nineteenth century."

VIII

CROSS-EYED SOULS

RECENTLY while reading a story in one of the current magazines I came across the expressive phrase "cross-eyed souls." It was used to describe those individuals who seem constitutionally unable to face the facts of life honestly. To become morally cross-eyed is comparatively easy. We are all somewhat inclined to see things as we want to see them instead of seeing them as they are. There are times when it takes genuine courage to look squarely at a disagreeable situation. The man who tries to ignore the truth sooner or later will reach a place where he cannot distinguish between the true and the false. Lies begin at home; the liar first deceives himself. And woe to that man who has so abused his gift of vision that he cannot tell light from darkness. "If thine eye be full of darkness, thy whole body is full of darkness." John Burroughs has written an essay entitled "Straight Seeing and Straight Thinking."

Straight thinking depends upon straight seeing, and a man always lives as he thinks.

Seeing is a psychological as well as a physio-
logical process. The same object brings decidedly different pictures to different minds.
Two men enter a library. One sees simply
row after row of books, while the heart of the
other leaps within him as he recognizes upon
the shelves friends, well tried and true. The
geologist can read the history of prehistoric
æons where the rest of us see nothing but a
few stones. As the train glides over the mountains, glowing with the ineffable beauty of the
dying summer day, to the poet the autumn-
tinted hills bring visions of apocalyptic splendor, but the gum-chewing, vacuous-voiced group
across the aisle behold only trees and rocks.
To some the sad-faced, toil-worn woman as
she plods wearily along is only another unin-
teresting member of the human race, but
those who can really see read upon that wrinkled
face "Sweet records promises as sweet."

The richness and the fullness of our lives is in
proportion to our power to see. To have eyes
and to see not is to live a half life.

John Ruskin has written these ultraemphatic
but entirely truthful words: "The more I
think of it the more I find this conclusion
impressed upon me, that the greatest thing a

human soul ever does in this world is to see
something and tell what it saw in a plain way,
Hundreds of people can talk for one who can
think, but thousands can think for one who
can see." Sometimes the eloquent words of
Ruskin are almost as hopeless as the wailings
of a Cassandra among the flames of Troy.
But whether they be optimistic or pessimistic.
facts are facts. The number of those who
positively will not see is anything but small.
There is no royal road to truth of any kind.
To learn really to see is not the easiest of
lessons. Truth can be attained only by those
who dare to scale the cold and rugged heights.
It is easy for prejudice or selfishness to blind
the eye of man.

Several years ago a newspaper, in chronicling the demise of one who had taken too
much opium, appeared with an article headed,
"Died of an Overdose of Opinion." Printer's
errors must not, of course, be taken too seri-
ously. But if "an overdose of opinion" were
fatal, many of us who are to-day in the land
of the living would have long since shuffled
off this mortal coil. The world is full of well-
meaning people who pronounce offhand judgments upon the gravest and most complicated
matters. The oracles of the village grocery
and barber shop are most militantly cocksure

in regard to the problems of labor and capital, the management of armies and navies, and the conduct of government at home and abroad. There are those who read nothing but the headlines and the sporting page, who do not hesitate to discourse learnedly upon the gravest of international questions. It is the immature student who knows the most about curriculums and discipline. Ignorance is always dogmatic.

The truth-seeker and the truth-finder are always openminded. All knowledge which man wins is a revealer of new fields lying in the distance. Books which in other years were regarded as ultimate wisdom to-day gather dust upon library shelves. In many fields of intellectual activity the more light, the less certainty. The great scholar is tolerant; the unilluminated grammarian regards the printed word of the pedant as final, worthy to be written upon tables of stone. Ignorance is dogmatic in regard to its own viewpoint and full of contemptuous pity for all who differ with it. It is easy to have essentially the same attitude toward life as the old lady who in a discussion of church unity amiably remarked: "What's the use of having so many denominations? Why can't everybody be sensible and be a Methodist?" Dogmatism means intellectual blindness. Truth cannot be really attained by those who view it from only one side. "Dearly beloved brethren," expostulated Oliver Cromwell with a group of dogmatic clericals, "I beseech you by the mercies of God to realize that you may be mistaken." In all of the fields of human endeavor there are still untold mysteries. We but know in part. We see only through a glass darkly. Absolute knowledge is not the portion of man. In the presence of the vast unknown it is for the children of men to walk humbly with open minds and receptive hearts.

Sometimes there is a great gulf fixed between what we want to do and what we ought to do. There is always a danger of our substituting desire for duty. We are tempted even to allow our inclinations to mold our principles. When we do wrong our tendency is to make excuses. Therefore we are prone to adapt our ethics to our deeds. But there is always hope for an honest man. No matter how many mistakes one has made, if he is sincere enough and brave enough to acknowledge his errors, he has not entirely lost the right path.

The degeneration of a soul is the most gripping and heartrending of human tragedies. Spiritual disaster comes not in an hour. In the West Indies there is an insect which eats out the heart of a pillar while it is to all appearances sound. Tampering with one's loyalty to truth has a subtle but certain disintegrating influence upon the character and personality. It may be that in a moment of unguarded weakness sin enters a life. But God is ever merciful; the door of the Father's house is never closed to the poor prodigal. Yet the man who in order to justify his wrongdoings refuses to acknowledge them to be sins, closes the door of hope upon himself. The prodigal who makes himself believe that the licentious life of the far country is manly and honorable journeys farther and farther from the lights of home.

Oscar Wilde, a man from whose life others walked backward with averted gaze, once said, "I remember when I was at Oxford saying to one of my friends as we were strolling around Magdalen's narrow, bird-haunted walks one morning in the year before I took my degree, that I wanted to eat of the fruit of all the trees in the garden of the world and, that I was going out into the world with that passion in my soul." Wilde tried to justify his sin by giving expression to a noxious, mephitic philosophy of life. But sin is sin and cannot be purified by paragraphs of vapid, high-sounding words.

"If you must, be a pig
   In and out of season,
But do not justify it with a big
   Philosophic reason."

Cut in the stone above the chancel in the
chapel of one of the historic American pre-
paratory schools, in the words of the heroic
Apostle to the Gentiles is the motto of the
institution, "Whatsoever things are true." A
life philosophy built around these words will
always ring true. Emerson said, "The world
is upheld by the veracity of good men; they
make the earth wholesome." The materialism
of which Thomas Henry Huxley was the chief
protagonist is to-day without defenders. But
Huxley himself is still a potent influence. His
life, written by his son, is a biography which
no alert, idealistic youth can afford to leave
unread. The tremendous influence of this
Victorian scientist is due to his unswerving
devotion to truth. His son and biographer
writes, "If wife and child," he said, "were
all lost to me, one after another, I would
not lie."

A number of years ago the editor of a great
American newspaper was in Paris. The question arose as to whether the paper should join
the party with which it was allied in support-
ing a policy which this publication had for

years opposed. To break with the party meant loss, perhaps bankruptcy. A cable was sent to the old chief in Paris. Without delay came the answer, "Never compromise with dishonor." Faithfulness to truth in the abstract is easy, but a man is to be measured by his attitude toward the concrete problems which he is called to face. Tampering with facts in order to make a case is sinning against one's soul. Truth must not be roughly handled. To see the truth, to speak it, and to act it with constancy and precision is one of the world's most difficult tasks. To gloss over realities in the name of a silly optimism is to sell the soul to the demons of falsehood. It is not a virtue to call black white. In one of Ruskin's noblest passages we read: "I do not mean to diminish the blame of the injurious and malicious sin of the selfish and deliberate falsity; yet it seems to me that the shortest way to check the darker forms of deceit is to set more scrupulous watch against those which have mingled, unregarded and unchastised, with the current of our life. Do not let us lie at all. Do not think of one falsity as harmless, and another as slight, and another as unintended. Cast them all aside; they may be light and accidental; but they are an ugly soot from the smoke of the pit for all that;

and it is better that our hearts should be swept
clean of them, without ever caring as to which
is the largest or blackest."

We can never afford to sacrifice principle to
expediency. Disloyalty to truth opens the door
for other sins. Each falsehood begets many
of its species. A nameless individual in trying
to justify certain questionable practices to
Samuel Johnson said, "A man must live."
"I don't see the necessity," blurted out the
sturdy old philosopher. The psalmist says,
"The heathen are sunk down in the pit they
made; in the net which they hid is their own
foot taken." He who for any reason whatsoever ignores the truth, digs a pit into which
he himself is doomed to fall sooner or later;
he hides a net in which his own feet eventually
become enmeshed. Horace Bushnell's sermons
mostly have epigrammatic titles which suggest
their central thought. One bears the caption,
"The Capacity for Religion Extirpated by
Disuse." It is true in general that any power
which is not used atrophies. "That which is
not expressed dies." The time comes when he
who will not see cannot see.

As the years take us farther away from the
nineteenth century we are able to discern that
among its other outstanding contributions to
the world of thought must be numbered its

bringing to the service of education, industry,
and government that temper of mind which
is known as scientific. It is entirely probable
that the scientific spirit as applied by intellectual neophytes to philosophy and literature
has been to a degree responsible for the arrant
foolishness of those who have tried to me-
chanicalize the spiritual. But above all else
it stands for a passion for truth. In a college
classroom where a student in attempting to
translate from a continental language into
English had on account of a ludicrous error
become the object of the derisive laughter of
the class, the professor remarked, "A guess
is a good thing, provided we guess right."
But, as a general rule, good guessing is based
on knowledge. No flight of the imagination
can take the place of a grasp of facts. The
scientific temper means a love of truth and a
hatred of falsehood. It means a willingness
to face realities whether or not they accord
with our prejudices or our interests.

Amiel has made the striking statement that
"The number of beings who wish to see truly
is extraordinarily small." Whether this is an
exaggeration or not, it is certainly true that
no one ever sees clearly without wishing to see
clearly. It is easy to quote Burns's rollicking
lines:

"O wad some power the giftie gie us
    To see oursel's as others see us!
    It wad frae monie a blunder free us,
        And foolish notion."

It may be, however, that others do not see us
exactly as we are. Dr. Holmes, in the guise of
the autocrat, showed how one of his table
companions, "a young fellow answering to the
name of John," had three distinct personalities:

THREE JOHNS

1. The real John; known only to his Maker.
2. John's ideal John; never the real one and often very
   unlike him.
3. Thomas's ideal John; never the real John, nor
   John's John, but very often unlike either.

The result of learning to know our real
selves might not always be to the highest
degree flattering. But without self-knowledge
there can be no growth. A self-revealing mistake may be a powerful incentive to progress.
He who dares to know the truth walks in the
light. A zeal for doing which is not allied
with a passion for knowing is, to say the least,
fraught with grave social perils. The last
words of Goethe were, "Light! more light!"
In an age of new problems, of industrial, political, and social chaos, when with phenomenal
rapidity the old order yields place to the new,

when we know not whither the tides of life are hurling us, the outstanding need of our generation is a clear and broad vision of the fundamental verities. The knowing of the truth is not always inevitably followed by the doing of the right. But without a firm grasp of essential truth there can be no progress, either individual or social. The first and greatest service that a human being can render to society is to be wholeheartedly honest with himself.

IX

THE AMERICAN HERITAGE

RACIALLY we Americans are a cosmopolitan people, but our spiritual heritage is of Anglo-Saxon lineage. It has come to us through the men who upon the rock-bound coast of New England and by the sloping banks of the rivers of old Virginia laid the foundations of future States. From the very first the gates of this new land "beyond the ocean bars" have been open to all light-seeking, truth-loving sons of men. The thirteen colonies long before the Revolution were inhabited by men and women of more than one race. In New York were the sturdy descendants of the unconquerable men of Holland, than whom no race has fought nobler battles for human liberty. In New Jersey and in Delaware were those who in memory still climbed the snowy hills of Sweden and heard her Sabbath bells. In the South, and even among the Puritans of New England, dwelt those of French names in whose veins coursed the blood of the Huguenots, who for the sake of their fathers' faith, became fugitives and wanderers upon the face of the earth. In the Quaker Commonwealth of William Penn, along with the peaceful Friend from English hedgerows and green Irish meadows, there dwelt men of Teutonic blood from the legend-haunted valley of the Rhine and the snowy peaks and hoary glaciers of liberty-loving Switzerland. And there too glowed the fire of Celtic hearts. In more than one sequestered vale even to-day the old Welsh names tell of those of the faith of Pennsylvania's founder who brought with them to the American wilderness the tradition of the storied hills and rugged mountains of little Wales. And beyond the blue ridges of the Alleghanies the militant dauntless Ulster Scot faced the terrors of the wilderness and led the westward march of empire. No part of these United States can trace its ancestry to one race alone. Neither are we a mere conglomerate of many races. We are a new people—not English, nor Irish, nor German, nor French, but Americans.

In Bayard Taylor's "National Ode," read upon Independence Square, Philadelphia, July 4, 1876, just once does the poet rise to the level of the momentous day and the memorable occasion. In speaking of his country he said:

"No blood in her lightest veins
Frets at remembered chains,
No shame nor bondage has bowed her head.
In her form and features still
The unblenching Puritan will,
Cavalier honor, Huguenot grave,
The Quaker truth and sweetness,
And the strength of the danger-girdled race
Of Holland, blend in a proud completeness.
From the homes of all, where her being began.
. . . .
Her Germany dwells by a gentler Rhine;
Her Ireland sees the old sunburst shine;
Her France pursues some dream divine;
Her Norway keeps his mountain pine;
Her Italy waits by the western brine;
And broad-based under all
Is planted England's oaken-hearted mood,
As rich in fortitude
As e'er went worldward from the island-wall!
Fused in her candid light,
To one strong race all races here unite."

Here the poet, in language succinct and beautiful, gives expression to a fundamental fact of our national life. We are of many extractions, but "one people with one language, the English language, and one flag, the American flag." Many tributaries have flowed into the river of our American thought and ideals, but its source is unmistakably English. Whatever our race or sign, we are fundamentally Anglo-Saxon.

We are heirs of the "great tradition" of the Anglo-Saxon line.   It was for us that the sturdy barons at Runnymede wrested the Great Charter from a weak-kneed tyrant.   It was for us that Cromwell and his Ironsides waged heroic warfare at Naseby and Marston Moor. It was for us that Burke in winged words uttered his burningly eloquent defense of the ancient English liberties.   It was to protect these selfsame inalienable rights that American yeomen laid down their lives at Bunker Hill and Brandywine.   But our political heritage is but a slender portion of the priceless inheritance which has come to us from beneath the somber skies of Old England.

To be thankful that the English language is our language indicates no spirit of provincial narrowness.   So indissolubly is our speech united with the best in our national life that he whose inner life is most adequately expressed in another language and speaks in a foreign tongue and glorifies it at the expense of our national vernacular is fundamentally a foreigner.   One lesson of the war which cannot be ignored is that the easier we make it for new citizens to retain the dialects and languages of lands across the water, the harder will be the task of Americanization.   To have for our national speech the language whose

line has gone out to the uttermost parts of the
earth, which to-day comes the nearest to being really a world language, is not the least
of our national blessings. And through our
linguistic heritage our soul lives are deepened
and broadened by contact with the noblest
body of literature ever produced by any people
in the annals of the human race. In speech
at least Chaucer, Shakespeare, Milton, Wordsworth, Tennyson, and Browning are of us.
This kinship in the starlit realms of literature
with those who until the latest days will
tower like sunken continents above oblivion's
sea has in it something which should cast at
least a faint "gleam" upon the barren fields
of the most sordid and commonplace day.

Mighty as may be the appeal to the American heart of the supreme literature of the
seagirt motherland, it is in the literary work
of our own country that we find most clearly
reflected our national life and ideals. Sometimes a poet or novelist brings us far nearer
to the heart of reality than the historian or
philosopher. It is futile to discuss the silly
academic question as to whether or not there is a
distinctive American literature. The flowers of
prose and poetry which have sprung from
American soil are American and nothing else.
In the literature of our nation we find mir-

rored forth our history and our outstanding
characteristics.

What are the qualities of mind and heart
which differentiate Americans from other races
of the human species? In the make-up of
the "cosmopolitanly planned" citizen of this
great new land are there ingredients which are
new under the sun, or do we represent a new
combination of human traits as old as the
world? It does not take a vast amount of
thinking to come to the conclusion that the
latter question is the one which compels an
affirmative answer. A great seer once said,
"Mankind progresses; man ever remains the
same." But it is worth while to notice a few
of those elements of human nature which loom
largest in the American mind and character.

1. The real American is democratic. He
rates a man according to his own merits rather
than upon the height of his family tree. He
believes that there is a real greatness latent in
the commonest of the children of men. With
Burns he says:

> "The rank is but the guinea's stamp,
>   The man's the gowd for a' that."

It must, of course, be admitted that there are
within the borders of these United States
some representatives of that species which

Thackeray excoriated under the name of snob.
But the would-be aristocrat and the real
American can never dwell in the same tenement of clay. The American is open, frank,
and free, both approaching and approachable.
It has been said that the English people are
like their own ale, "froth on top, dregs at the
bottom, but sound in the middle." This
description is by no means inapplicable to
our own people. It must, moreover, be remembered that the froth of humanity is just
as worthless as the dregs. Among the froth
of American life there are arrant snobs, and
at the bottom we find the braying Bolshevist.
But between these two extremes are solidity,
strength, and real democracy. We can judge
a people by their national heroes. Abraham
Lincoln, who, as the years go by, is being
more and more legendized and idealized, was
simply "one of the folks." The plain frame
house in Springfield which he left for the
White House was a simple, typical American
home. He was too big a man to have any
place in his make-up for superficial, adventitious
standards of judging his fellow men. And
this characteristic of Lincoln is one of the
distinctive marks of Americanism. In his
outstanding essay on "Democracy," Lowell
says that the democratic method is "such an

organization of society as will enable men to respect themselves."

It must be remembered that nowhere else do we come into such vital touch with the life of a people as upon the pages of their literature. There is a profound significance in the fact that our American literature is essentially democratic. It is true that there is an element of insularity in the literature of the New England renaissance. For some of the writers of that period Boston was verily "the hub of the solar system." But Longfellow, saturated as he was with the culture of the Old World, sang of the natural sorrows, losses, and joys which go to make up the common life of everyday men and women. Emerson stands out with translucent clearness as the great interpreter of our national democracy. He was limited in powers of human contact but catholic in his sympathy. In the literature of the older day the only place in which we find the democratic spirit lacking is in the writings of Dr. Holmes. No poetry is more distinctively American than that of Whittier, who wrote about common people for common people. Our American writers have not dealt with kings and barons, legendary or real. Upon their pages we do not come into contact with supermen or titanic amazons, but with men and women to whom we are drawn as it were by cords invisible because they are delightfully human. And the same note of sincere democracy is sounded in the most distinctive writings of our own day. As we travel "North of Boston" with Robert Frost "Old hearths grow wide to make us room" as truly as did the old fireplace in the Whittier kitchen at Haverhill. In Masters and Sandburg we feel the mighty pulsations of the broad, free Middle West without knowing which no man can know America. It is not at all certain that when the mists of the present have rolled away we shall not come to see that in the writings of Walt Whitman, Mark Twain, and William Dean Howells we get nearer to the heart of American life than in any history which has been or will be written. Our national literature is redolent of green meadows and running brooks, of broad fields, of tree-embowered villages and the thronging streets of the busy city. Everywhere it is permeated with "the folksiness of the folks." American literature is democratic because American life is democratic.

2. Americans are a practical, achieving people. Our feet are always on the ground. By their fruits we judge them. We believe in "The nobility of labor—the long pedigree of toil."

The Rooseveltian doctrine that idleness is criminality is a thought near the center of the typical American philosophy of life. Walt Whitman in "I hear America singing" images the poetry of common toil:

"The shoemaker singing as he sits at his bench,
The hatter singing as he stands,
The delicious singing of the mother or of the young wife
At work, or the girl sewing or washing,
Each singing what belongs to him or her and to none else."

Whittier's "Songs of Labor" gives us a virile American note and Dr. Henry van Dyke in his "Toiling of Felix" in lines of gentle beauty says[1]:

"Blessed are they that labor, for Jesus partakes of their bread,
He puts his hand to their burdens, he enters their homes at night:
Who does his best shall have as his guest, the Master of life and light.

"This is the gospel of labor, ring it ye bells of the kirk!
The Lord of Love came down from above, to live with the men who work.
This is the rose that he planted, here in the thorn-curst soil;
Heaven is blest with perfect rest, but the blessing of earth is toil."

---

[1] Printed by permission of Charles Scribner's Sons, Publishers.

The old monk's motto, *Laborare est orare*, does not need to be explained to the typical American. He not only believes it but he lives it. Our religion is intensely practical. The mysticism of our fathers has faded into the light of common day. Even in our spiritual lives we have become somewhat of the earth earthy. Of course in almost every community can be found the canting hypocrite who substitutes the mechanical performance of mechanical rites for doing justice, loving mercy, and walking humbly with the Master. But in general the efficacy of a man's religion is measured by his loyalty to duty and his integrity in his dealings with his fellow men. From our present-day viewpoint the criterion of the effectiveness of anything is workability. We have no time for theories. We minimize creeds. We are too practical to be concerned with the fundamental. Sometimes we are ready to start on a journey before the road is built. In fact, we have a tendency to push right on without bothering to inform ourselves as to our destination. James and Dewey with their pragmatism have brought philosophy from the clouds to the world of men. "If it works, it's true." "This," says the metaphysician, "is not philosophy. It is but a wild-goose chase." His contention may be

true. But somehow, Professor James and
his followers have told us something which we
have all vaguely felt before anyone brought
it to the surface and put it into words. At
least they have formulated ideas which have
long been in the atmosphere of our land and
age.

Our practicality naturally has the defects
of its qualities. We are not a reverent people.
Nothing upon earth or in the heavens above
the earth or in the waters under the earth is
safe from the jesting Yankee. Mark Twain's
lack of reverence is typically American. Then,
too, it cannot be denied that our practical-
ness has tended to make us materialistic.
But at all events we are no "idle dreamers
of an empty day." In our faith there is no
room for dead scholasticism or barren asceticism. And, after all, we are by no means
deaf to the appeal of a noble idealism. We
insist, however, upon our ideals being translated into deeds. We are not satisfied with
perfect theories in the closet. We demand
those which will stand the test of the market
place. Like Bunyan's hero, "Life, more life!"
is our cry.

3. The American is an instinctive pioneer.
Even in the oldest parts of our country we are
a new people, the children of immigrants.

This is not without significance in the study
of our national characteristics. He who leaves
the home of his fathers for a new land is mostly
an adventurous soul, who longs to find that
which is "lost behind the ranges." The history of the three centuries of life upon this
continent is essentially the story of the pioneer.
The conquest of the land between ocean and
ocean is a veritable Odyssey of the frontier.
What a mighty drama of history is compressed
into Walt Whitman's vivid lines!—

"All the past we leave behind,
  We debouch upon a newer, mightier world, varied world,
  Fresh and strong the world we seize, world of labor and
    the march,
        Pioneers! Pioneers!

"We detachments steady throwing,
  Down the edges, through the passes, up the mountains
    steep,
  Conquering, holding, daring, venturing as we go the
    unknown ways,
        Pioneers! Pioneers!

"All the pulses of the world,
  Falling in they beat for us, with the Westward move-
    ment beat,
  Holding single or together, steady moving to the front,
    all for us,
        Pioneers! Pioneers!"

Roosevelt's Winning of the West, Churchill's
The Crossing, and other books which tell of

the westward march of Anglo-Saxon civilization are replete with tales of dauntless heroism. America has always faced the future.

As a people we are not inclined to linger around the sunken reefs of the past. Spiritually as well as physically we are of pioneer stock. In The American Scholar Emerson says, "The eyes of a man are set in his forehead, not in his hindhead." And again: "Our day of dependence, our long apprenticeship to the learning of other lands, draws to a close. The millions that around us are rushing into life, cannot always be fed upon the sere remains of foreign harvests." Emerson's doctrine of self-reliance, although "sicklied o'er" with a nebulous Kantean transcendentalism, is intrinsically American. He is preeminently the prophet of individualism. "Trust thyself," he says, "every heart vibrates to that iron string." In America we find not types but individuals. That "goosestep efficiency" which was so much vaunted before 1914 was always a plant of slow growth upon this side of the Atlantic.

We are not slavish imitators of those who have gone before, although it cannot be said that we have refused to avail ourselves of the lessons of the past. The windows of our hearts and minds are ever open to new light and new truth. We are not afraid of the untrodden

pathway. We believe that a man's creed—
political, social, or religious—is not something
that can be slipped on or off like a raincoat.
It has to do with the life within. It cannot
unchanged be transmitted from one generation to another. Possibly there is no American poem which makes a wider appeal to
the idealism of college students than Lowell's
"The Present Crisis." Never does a year pass
without its being quoted many times in some
undergraduate oration. Lines like these strike
an answering chord in the heart of the twentieth
century college boy:

"'Tis as easy to be heroes as to sit the idle slaves
Of a legendary virtue carved upon our fathers' graves,
Worshipers of light ancestral make the present light a
    crime—
Was the Mayflower launched by cowards, steered by men
    behind their time?
Turn those tracks toward Past or Future, that make
    Plymouth Rock sublime?
.   .   .   .
"New occasions teach new duties; Time makes ancient
    good uncouth;
They must upward still and onward, who would keep
    abreast of Truth;
Lo, before us gleam her camp-fires! We ourselves must
    Pilgrims be,
Launch our Mayflower, and steer boldly through the
    desperate winter sea,
Nor attempt the Future's portal with the Past's blood-
    rusted key."

In such words the American speaks.

4. The American is a patriot. When he quotes Daniel Webster and says, "I was born an American; I will live an American, and I will die an American," he is not uttering mere words. Edward Everett Hale's little story The Man Without a Country expresses an idea which is deeply rooted in our national life. It is seldom indeed that a citizen of the United States transfers his allegiance to any other country. There may be a scintilla of truth in Samuel Johnson's definition of patriotism as "the last refuge of a scoundrel." In speaking of his country it is easy for an insincere man eloquently to utter labored nothings. But more than once has the soul of America been tried in the grim crucible of war. On many a battle-torn field her sons have died to uphold her honor. During long years of peace the fires of patriotism have brightly burned upon our national altars. It must, however, be admitted that there are in America those whose hearts have never thrilled with the noble emotion which we call "love of country." The life-detached intellectualist proudly proclaims himself an internationalist and refers to love of one's native land as "baby patriotism." A large section of the foreign-language press is shadowed with an

intangible but ever-present hyphenism. There are American citizens of foreign birth or immediate descent who very frequently, for reasons of "loaves and fishes," make systematic efforts to impede the Americanization of those to whom they are affiliated by race, by conducting propaganda in favor of foreign languages and foreign customs. In addition we must reckon with the anti-social teaching which especially since the war has been disseminated throughout the country. It is also apparent that in those magazines which to-day find nothing in the world worthy of commendation outside of Germany, Bolshevist Russia, and Sinn-Fein Ireland, the American note is very conspicuous by its absence. But in spite of these obnoxious manifestations the rank and file of American manhood and womanhood in the truest and noblest sense of the word are patriotic. The crowds who in the summer throng into the Chautauqua tents in almost every town and village have no tolerance for disloyalty in any form. The noise which hyphenism makes causes us to overestimate the number in the ranks of the malcontents. It is true that there must be no compromise with this type of dishonor, that we must lose no opportunity to check and counteract poisonous propaganda. We still,

however, can quote with assurance Longfellow's lines written in a much darker hour
than the present:

"Thou, too, sail on, O Ship of State!
Sail on, O UNION, strong and great!
.   .   .   .
Fear not each sudden sound and shock,
'Tis of the wave and not the rock;
'Tis but the flapping of the sail,
And not a rent made by the gale!
In spite of rock and tempest's roar,
In spite of false lights on the shore,
Sail on, nor fear to breast the sea!
Our hearts, our hopes are all with thee,
Our hearts, our hopes, our prayers, our tears,
Our faith triumphant o'er our fears,
Are all with thee—are all with thee!"

5. Idealism is a dominant American characteristic. When Arthur Balfour was on his
visit to this country he said, "Because America
was commercial it was easy to suppose that
she was materialistic." "We are," ex-President
Eliot, of Harvard, says, "the most idealistic
people who have thus far inherited the planet.
We are more idealistic in our conception of
man, of God, and of the universe than any
other people." It was a great ideal which
sent the little Mayflower across the wintry
sea. Men and women who are for the sake
of their faith willing to break all of the precious

ties uniting them to the land of their fathers
represent the quintessence of idealism.   The
Pilgrim Fathers endured as seeing Him who
is invisible.   They looked beyond the transient
to the eternal.   "Their palaces were houses
not made with hands; their diadems crowns
of glory which should never fade away."   As
Moses Coit Tyler has eloquently told us,
before the stumps were brown in their earliest
harvest field or the wolves had ceased to howl
nightly around their habitation they founded
schools and colleges.   In speaking of the first
of these embryo colleges Dr. Holmes says:

> "And when at length the College rose,
>   The sachem cocked his eye
> At every tutor's meager ribs
>   Whose coat-tails whistled by;
> But when the Greek and Hebrew words
>   Came tumbling from his jaws,
> The copper-colored children all
>   Ran screaming to the squaws.

> "And who was on the Catalogue
>   When College was begun?
> Two nephews of the President,
>   And *the* Professor's son;
> (They turned a little Indian by,
>   As brown as any bun;)
> Lord! how the seniors knocked about
>   The freshman class of one!"

But these little colleges on the seaboard were
the expression of the same dauntless idealism
which brought their founders across the sea.
And these English Dissenters who planted on
the barren New England the seeds of a new
civilization have been beyond the peradventure
of a doubt the most potent factors in the
spiritual history of the American people.

During the centuries that have passed, sons
and daughters of every land as they followed
the gleam have turned their steps toward
America, the land of the ideal. Americans have
never failed to hear the call of heroic service
and knightly deeds. We as a people have
learned that man does not live by bread alone.
There have been times in American history
when it has seemed as though ideals were
upon the scaffold and materialism upon the
throne. That period of American history between Lincoln and Roosevelt does not make
especially inspiring reading. The sublime idealism which manifested itself in the Civil War
reacted into sordidness and greed. But there
never has been a time of no vision. Even
days of darkness are illumined by some of the
noblest names in our history. It is not without significance that Ralph Waldo Emerson,
who more than any mirrored forth in his
writings the life and thought of the first cen-

tury of our national existence, was preeminently an idealist. "Do not," he said, "leave the sky out of your landscape." Another daring figure which thrills with the real Emersonian idealism is the often-quoted but never thread-bare aphorism, "Hitch your wagon to a star." We are the sons of men and women who cherished ideals, who stood for the purity of the home, for personal integrity, for social helpfulness, and for a vital sense of the life of God in the soul of man. We belong to a generation which with no blot of selfishness upon our escutcheon helped to wage a great war. As a people and as individuals it is for us to conserve our honor, truth, and righteous-ness. The gleam that never was on land or sea must not be allowed to fade into the light of common day.

Olympus cannot be crushed into a nut-shell. The complex life of over a hundred million people cannot adequately be synthe-sized in a few paragraphs. Each American is not like every other American. We live in the land of magnificent distances, in an environ-ment which develops rather than represses individuality. But our differences are more obvious than real. Superficially we are heterogeneous, but fundamentally we are alike. Beneath the surface differences and the in-

evitable distinctions arising from varying hered-
itary and environistic influences are found the
traits which characterize the American.   As
the wheels of time make their ceaseless revolu-
tions "The thoughts of man are widened with
the process of the suns."   We have not yet
scaled the highest mountain nor placed our
banner upon its loftiest peak.   We must not
be satisfied with the virtues of our fathers.
The American of to-morrow must be bigger
and better than the American of to-day.

Every experience is a key which opens the
doors of life to newer and richer experiences.
We stand upon the shoulders of our fathers.
To equal them we must surpass them.   The
problems of to-day must not be faced in any
despicable spirit of "after us the deluge."   It
is for us to pass the torch of idealism from the
generations which have come and gone to
those which are yet to be.

X

PERMANENT VALUES IN THE
BIGLOW PAPERS

In American literature in the field of satire we have nothing better to show than Lowell's Biglow Papers. They deal with the living issues of a vital period of our history. The series of 1846–1848 gave expression to the deeply rooted opposition which existed to the Mexican War especially in New England, while that of 1862–1868 naturally reflects the tumultuous days of the Civil War. These satires are keen, brilliant, and racy. Hosea Biglow, the forthright, hard-headed, exuberantly witty Yankee philosopher, is in himself a contribution to literature. Above all else the Biglow Papers are American. They could not have been written outside of New England. They savor not of the library but of the soil. Lowell knew the Yankee's mind as well as his dialect. It is not hard for us to understand the popularity of these satires with the generation for whom they were written. But taking them in their entirety they are not especially inspiring to the reader of to-day. It is hard for

a satire to win immortality. Most of us have
little concern with the political quarrels of our
grandfathers. Few care to lose themselves in
the intricacies of midnineteenth-century politics. Literary material weighted down with
the transient is not interesting to posterity.
The perennial interest of "The Courtin' " is
evidence of the gulf fixed between it and the
work as a whole.

Yet, buried in dialect and almost entirely
overwhelmed by comment upon forgotten controversies, there is a veritable Golconda of
sparkling wit and rugged wisdom hewn from
the quarries of life. The underlying thought
of the poems is now only of historic interest.
But the works are worth reading for their
by-products. Shrewd, aptly phrased epigrams,
which "Poor Richard" himself might have
coined are to be found on many otherwise
tedious pages. And here the student of Lowell
comes into contact with truths as vital and
dynamic to-day as when they first came
bounding from the rapid pen of the poet.

Words which have to do with loyalty to
principle do not deal with any evanescent
theme. More than one pungent stanza in
these poems satirizes cant and insincerity.
Lowell[1] makes the self-seeking politician say:

[1] The selections from Lowell are used by permission of Houghton
Mifflin Company, Publishers.

"I du believe in prayer an' praise
   To him thet hez the grantin'
O' jobs—in everythin' that pays,
   But most of all in CANTIN';
This doth my cup with marcies fill,
   This lays all thought o' sin to rest—
I *don't* believe in princerple,
   But oh, I *du* in interest."

Again we read:

"A marciful Providunce fashioned us holler
 O' purpose thet we might our princerples swaller;
It can hold any quantity on 'em, the belly can,
An' bring 'em ready fer use like the pelican,
Or more like the kangaroo, who (wich is stranger)
Puts her family into her pouch wen there's danger.
Ain't princerple precious? then who's goin' to use it
Wen there's resk o' some chap's gittin up to abuse it?
I can't tell the wy on't, but nothin' is *so* sure
Ez thet princerple kind o' gits spiled by exposure."

With a few slight changes the following stanza
would suit the self-seeking candidate of any
time or place:

"Ez to my princerples, I glory
   In hevin' nothin' o' the sort;
I ain't a Wig, I ain't a Tory,
   I'm jest a canderdate, in short;
Thet's fair an' square an' parpendicler,
   But, ef the Public cares a fig
To have me an' thin' in particler,
   Wy, I'm a kind o' peri-Wig."

It is also true that in some respects election
to Congress has about the same influence

upon some men to-day as it had in the time
of Hosea Biglow:

"So, wen one's chose to Congriss, ez soon ez he's in it,
  A collar goes right round his neck in a minit,
  An' sartin it is thet a man cannot be strict
  In bein' himself, wen he gits to the Deestrict,
  Fer a coat thet sets wal here in ole Massachusetts,
  Wen it gits on to Washinton, somehow askew sets."

Perhaps the most contemptible type of
hypocrite is the individual who eloquently
fulminates against wrong in general and skill-
fully avoids any reference to specific transgres-
sions of the laws of right. Some one has given
three rules which are to be followed if one is
to avoid making enemies: "Say nothing, do
nothing, be nothing." The opponent of wrong
in the abstract follows all three of these rules
and at the same time gulls many into believing him to be a valiant soldier in the army
of the common good. Sometimes the most
pusillanimous coward is loudest in his thunders
against remote wrong and distant sinners.
Lowell pays his respects to this form of hypocrisy in these lines of galling satire:

"I'm willin' a man should go tollable strong
  Agin wrong in the abstract, fer thet kind o' wrong
  Is ollers unpop'lar an' never gits pitied,
  Because it's a crime no one never committed;
  But he mus'n't be hard on partickler sins,
  Coz then he'll be kickin' the people's own shins."

Lowell had a Carlylean hatred of insincerity and he possessed the power of finding the weak places in the armor of those against whom he lifted his well-pointed lance.

Lowell's satire in the main concerns itself with politics, and, like much political writing, it is not especially characterized by fairness to those whom it criticizes. There are passages which impress us as simply shallow cleverness. Satire, nevertheless, has never been especially judicial. It is somewhat in the habit of taking sides. It was an utter impossibility for a red-blooded man like James Russell Lowell to be a colorless neutral. Right or wrong, he stood on his own feet, did his own thinking, and without hesitation or equivocation expressed his opinions in language which could not be misunderstood.

Lowell owed much more of his make-up to his mother, who was of an old Orkney family and a descendant of the ballad hero, Sir Patrick Spens, than he did to the sturdy New England house of Lowell. He was, nevertheless, highly conscious of his Puritan heritage. Whatever the faults of the Yankee Ironsides, they were no namby-pamby weaklings. They were indeed men of present valor, "stalwart old iconoclasts." This characteristic of the men who in New England and America struck

sledge-hammer blows for human freedom is
set forth in "Sunthin' in the Pastoral Line"
in the portrait of Hosea's "gret-gran'ther mul-
tiplied by three." Through the old Crom-
wellian, Lowell gives expression to more than
one sentiment permeated with wisdom and
strength. We read, for example, these words:

" 'Wal, milk-an'-water ain't the best o' glue,'
Sez he, 'an' so you'll find afore you're thru;
Ef rashness venters sunthin', shilly-shally
Loses ez often wut's ten times the vally.' "

And again in the same poem we find this ringing exhortation:

" 'Strike soon,' sez he, 'or you'll be deadly ailin'—
Folks thet's afeerd to fail are sure o' failin';
God hates your sneakin' creturs thet believe
He'll settle things they run away an' leave!' "

To discuss the lasting value of the Biglow
Papers without calling attention to the beautiful idyllic passages which take us near to
the very heart of New England would mean
the ignoring of some of the most charmingly
realistic pictures of rural life and landscape
to be found anywhere, except, possibly, upon
the pages of Whittier. Again "Sunthin' in
the Pastoral Line" yields rich treasure. For
example:

"Jes' so our spring gits everythin' in tune,
An' gives one leap from Aperl into June:
Then all comes crowdin' in; afore you think,
Young oak-leaves mist the side-hill woods with pink;
The catbird in the laylock-bush is loud;
The orchards turn to heaps o' rosy cloud;
Red-cedars blossom tu, though few folks know it,
An' look all dipt in sunshine like a poet;
The lime-trees pile their solid stacks o' shade
An' drows'ly simmer with the bees' sweet trade;
In ellum-shrouds the flashin' hangbird clings
An' for the summer vy'ge his hammock slings."

"Mason and Slidell: A Yankee Idyll" contains a vivid picture with an atmosphere all its own:

"I love to l'iter there while night grows still,
An' in the twinklin' villages about,
Fust here, then there, the well-saved lights goes out,
An' nary sound but watchdog's false alarms,
Or muffled cockcrows from the drowsy farms,
Where some wise rooster (men act jest thet way)
Stands to 't thet moon-rise is the break o' day."

There are few stanzas with more poetry to the line than in the opening words of "The Courtin' ":

"God makes sech nights, all white an' still,
Fur 'z you can look or listen,
Moonshine an' snow on field an' hill,
All silence an' all glisten."

In the apparently inexhaustible "Sunthin' in

the Pastoral Line" there is another stanza of real poetry which combines humor, suggestiveness, beauty, and inspiration:

"'T wuz so las' Sabbath arter meetin'-time:
  Findin' my feelin's wouldn't noways rhyme
  With nobody's, but off the hendle flew
  An' took things from an east-wind pint o' view,
  I started off to lose me in the hills
  Where the pines be, up back o' 'Siah's Mills;
  Pines, ef you're blue, are the best friends I know,
  They mope an' sigh an' sheer your feelin's so;
  They hesh the ground beneath so, tu, I swan,
  You half fergit you've gut a body on.
  Ther 's a small school'us there where four roads meet,
  The doorsteps hollered out by little feet,
  An' sideposts carved with names whose owners grew
  To gret men, some on 'em, an' deacons, tu;
  't ain't used no longer, coz the town hez gut
  A high school, where they teach the Lord knows wut:
  Three-story larnin' 's pop'lar now; I guess
  We thriv' 'ez wal on jes' two stories less,
  Fur it strikes me ther 's sech a thing ez sinnin'
  By overloadin' children's underpinnin';
  Wal, here it wuz I larned my A B C,
  An' it's a kind o' favorite spot with me."

In "A Yankee Idyll" is one of the poet's most vital and ringing stanzas. There is something wrong with the American who can read it without his heart beating faster. It is an Iliad of the frontier, an Odyssey of the wilderness:

"O strange New World, thet yit wast never young,
Whose youth from thee by gripin' need was wrung,
Brown foundlin' o' the woods, whose baby bed
Was prowled roun' by the Injun's cracklin' tread,
An' who grew'st strong thru shifts an' wants an' pains,
Nussed by stern men with empires in their brains,
Who saw in vision their young Ishmel strain
With each hard hand a vassal ocean's mane,
Thou, skilled by Freedom an' by gret events
To pitch new States ez Old-World men pitch tents,
Thou, taught by Fate to know Jehovah's plan
Thet man's devices can't unmake a man,
An' whose free latch-string never was drawed in
Against the poorest child of Adam's kin—
The grave's not dug where traitor hands shall lay
In fearful haste thy murdered corse away."

In spite of parlor-anarchists, hyphenates, Bolshevists, and other traitors these last lines may still be read with confident assurance.

To-day, better than we could a few years ago, we understand the tender pathos of these lines in which the love of winter beauty is overshadowed with an irrepressible longing for the dear, old, far-off days of peace:

"Where's Peace? I start, some clear-blown night,
    When gaunt stone walls grow numb an' number,
An', creakin' 'cross the snow-crus' white,
    Walk the col' starlight into summer;
Up grows the moon, an' swell by swell
    Thru the pale pasturs silvers dimmer
Than the last smile thet strives to tell
    O' love gone heavenward in its shimmer.

.   .   .   .

"Snowflakes come whisperin' on the pane,
    The charm makes blazin' logs so pleasant,
But I can't hark to wut they're say'n',
    With Grant or Sherman ollers present;

.   .   .   .

"Or up the slippery knob I strain
    An' see a hundred hills like islan's
Lift their blue woods in broken chain
    Out o' the sea o' snowy silence;
The farm-smokes, sweetes' sight on airth,
    Slow thru the winter air a-shrinkin',
Seem kin' o' sad, an' roun' the hearth
    Of empty places set me thinkin'."

It is not minimizing Lowell to say that he is by no means one of the great figures in the world's literature. But he has made contributions to our American letters without which we would be immeasurably poorer. It can also be said of him that no other writer has written in dialect lines so pathetically beautiful and enchantingly melodious.

But some of the pithiest lines in the two series are found detached from any other outstanding thought or expression. Consequently, many of them are all but lost to a very large proportion of modern readers. Yet these scintillating epigrams are replete with suggestions and homely common sense. Their name is legion, and the examples given are typical rather than inclusive:

"Democ'acy gives every man
The right to be his own oppressor."

"My gran'ther's rule was safer'n 't is to crow:
Don't never prophesy—onless ye know."

"(Why I'd give more for one bobolink
Than a square mile o' larks in printer's ink.)"

"Now don't go off half-cock; folks never gains
By usin' pepper-sarse instid o' brains."

"It's no use buildin' wut's a-goin to fall."

Here are two lines which each new generation
needs to remember:

"Young folks are smart, but all ain't good thet's new;
I guess the gran'thers they knowed sunthin' tu."

Few other writers could have expressed the
following thought without falling into banality
or irreverence:

"An' you've gut to git up airly
Ef you want to take in God."

In one of his satiric congressional speeches
two thoughts highly worthy of quotation are
sententiously expressed:

"But The'ry is jes' like a train on the rail,
Thet, weather or no, puts her thru without fail,
While Fac's the old stage thet gits sloughed in the ruts,
An' hez to allow for your darned efs an' buts,

.   .   .   .

An' folks don't want Fourth o' July t' interfere
With the business consarns o' the rest o' the year,
No more 'n they want Sunday to pry an' to peek
Into wut they are doin' the rest o' the week."

It would be hard to find an apter comment
upon certain phases of the Puritan character:

"Pleasure does make us Yankees kind o' winch,
    Ez though 't wuz sunthin' paid for by the inch;
    But yit we du contrive to worry thru,
    Ef Dooty tells us thet the thing's to du,
    An kerry a hollerday, ef we set out,
    Ez stiddily ez though 't wuz a redoubt."

Hume cynically remarked that the Puritans
hated bear-baiting not because it gave pain
to the bear, but because it gave pleasure to
the people.   This falsehood contained just
enough truth to make it effective.   Lowell's
lines express the truth of the aphorism of the
Scottish historian, but are without that which
made Hume's witticism palpably unjust.   More
than once has the New England satirist in this
fashion packed whole chapters of social psychology into a few pregnant sentences.

Another example of this is found in the
following lines from which no real student of
humanity will think of dissenting:

"An' yit I love th' unhighschooled way
    Ol' farmers hed when I wuz younger;
Their talk wuz meatier, an' 'ould stay
    While book-froth seems to wet your hunger;

For puttin' in a downright lick
   'twixt Humbug's eyes ther's few can metch it,
An' then it helves my thoughts ez slick
   Ez stret-grained hickory doos a hetchet."

In speaking of the Biglow Papers Charles Sumner said, "It's a pity that they are not written in the English language." Sumner represented that group of would-be super-intellectuals to whom writing in dialect is the committing of a sin against the most sacred literary conventionalities. Lowell's use of the Yankee dialect in the Biglow Papers enhanced their literary value because it gave them a closer contact with life. They are rooted in the very soil of New England. They give expression to the philosophy of an uncommon common man. Hosea Biglow is not a type but an individual. He has all of Lowell's own brilliancy and penetration. This was not true of every Yankee farmer, but it was true of some. The fact that Lowell had the dramatic power to express himself through such a rugged personality is not the least of the evidences of his title to a literary preeminence. This Harvard professor and exemplar of a rich cosmopolitan culture never lost his contact with the common things of life.

Lowell, like most of the towering figures of literature, again and again stressed certain dominant ideas. These are at the center of his teaching. In many instances these outstanding truths are expressed time after time in the two series of dialect poems. The presence of wit does not mean the absence of wisdom. In one of his essays he speaks of those individuals who "have been sent into the world unfurnished with the modulating and restraining balance wheel which we call a sense of humor."

To this group all work of humor is vanity and vexation of spirit. Others, however, in the Biglow Papers will come into contact with some of the ripest, richest, and most virile thoughts in American literature. In these poems we find more of Lowell than in any other work that came from his pen.

XI

LESSENING THE DENOMINATOR

It is in Sartor Resartus that we read the somewhat enigmatic sentence: "The Fraction of Life can be increased in value not so much by increasing your Numerator as by lessening your Denominator." Few men have made a more consistent effort to do this than Henry David Thoreau. Walden is the story of a sincere effort to increase the value of life by lessening the denominator. The book is drawn from a journal which the eccentric naturalist kept during the two years in which he lived in the shanty on the banks of Walden Pond. The book is interesting not so much because it tells of the author's ability to support himself upon the princely sum of seventeen cents a week, but rather on account of its giving expression to a luminous and distinctively individualistic philosophy of life.

The life of Thoreau could not be taken as a model. It was egoistic rather than social. After his death his friend and mentor, Emerson, wrote of him: "He was bred to no pro-

fession; he never married; he never voted;
he refused to pay a tax to the State; he ate no
flesh, he drank no wine; he never knew the use
of tobacco; and, though a naturalist, he used
neither trap nor gun." Not all of these devi-
ations from the typical life of his generation
can be looked upon as virtues. For most of
us Thoreau's two years of existence in the
woods would not be ideal. After Whittier read
the book he pronounced it "capital reading,"
but continued, "The practical moral of it seems
to be that if a man is willing to sink himself
into a woodchuck he can live as cheaply as
that quadruped; but, after all, for me, I prefer
walking on two legs." Such a reaction is easy
to understand, but it is, nevertheless, decidedly
unjust. The central thought of the volume is
found in the words: "A man is rich in proportion to the number of things which he can
afford to let alone." Brander Matthews says
Walden is a "most wholesome warning to all
those who are willing to let life itself be smoth-
ered out of them by luxuries they have allowed
to become necessaries."

In one of the cleverest, but unfairest essays
which came from his pen, Lowell without
mercy excoriates Thoreau and his philosophy
of life. But in spite of himself, Lowell gets to
the heart of the significance of the Walden

experiment and admits that its "aim was a
noble and useful one in the direction of plain
living and high thinking." It was a protest
against the tendency of the American to become the slave of his possessions. The story
is told that a friend attempted to present
Thoreau with a mat to be placed in front of
the door of the Walden hut, but he unhesi-
tatingly refused it. He said that by wiping
his feet on the grass he could save himself
the trouble of taking care of another article.
Henry Thoreau may have been an extremist.
However, it is possible that it would be better
for an individual to follow his example rather
than to make himself the slave of a clutter
of a conglomerate of objects neither beautiful
nor useful. It was not many years ago that
the largest and best-located room in the
American home was filled with haircloth furni-
ture, crayon portraits in hideous frames, and
other æsthetic monstrosities, and then merci-
fully closed for about three hundred and sixty-
four days of the year; but visited frequently by
the industrious housewife, who must keep her
treasures free from the defiling presence of
dust. Even to-day thousands of American
women are the servants of their dwelling
places. More than one life has been shortened
by utterly useless labor. Walden is a sermon

against the sin of Marthaism. A person "troubled about many things" has no time to master the art of living.

Thoreau has been criticized because instead of making money by manufacturing lead pencils, he took time to enjoy life in his own peculiar way. He could say like Walt Whitman,

"I loaf and invite my soul."

It must be admitted that not every loafer invites his soul to be a partner in his enterprises. The typical American, however, is likely to be too busy to realize that he is a being fundamentally spiritual. "Young people," said a college professor to one of his classes, "you look as though you spent twice as much time studying as you should." The jaded-looking group perceptibly brightened, but he continued as follows, "But you recite as though you did not spend half enough time at your books." It is easy indeed to be tremendously busy doing nothing. In Chaucer's Prolog there is a typical and delightful couplet in which the poet says of one of his characters,

"Nowher so busy as a man as he ther nas,
And yet he seemed bisier than he was."

A life can be buried beneath futile details, Richard Brinsley Sheridan gives some good

advice when he says, "Now and then be idle;
sit and think." No more precious gift is
intrusted to our stewardship than that of time.
A man's very soul may be entombed beneath a
mountain of trivialities. Efficiency depends not
only upon knowing what to do, but also upon
a knowledge of what to leave undone. He
who allows trifles to dominate his life narrows
his vision and impedes his usefulness. Ex-
treme busyness is America's besetting sin.
The securing of leisure is not only a privilege
but a duty. Thoreau at least mastered those
elements of truth which the world contained
for his especial acquisition. The writing of at
least one volume which has an assured place
among the classics of American literature
would alone be a fairly creditable showing for
a life of little more than forty years. How
many of Thoreau's merciless critics have that
much to their credit?

Diogenes once said, "Lord, I thank thee
that there are so many things which Diogenes
can do without." It is, indeed, easy for a
man to allow himself to be made the slave of
things. The "high cost of living" presents a
problem that is decidedly real, but by its side
is the equally vital question of the cost of
"high living." In the American life of to-day
it would be hard to draw the line between

that which is spent on pleasure or luxury and that spent on display. Sometimes we buy to please Mrs. Grundy. Our richer neighbor has something, and therefore we must have it, whether we can afford it or not. This fearful and merciless competition in the possession of things has for decades been one of the baneful influences of modern life. Thoreau says: "The cost of a thing is the amount of what I will call life, which is required to be exchanged for it, immediately or in the long run." Many times the price of display or luxury has meant the sacrificing of the higher values of life. For our own generation there is a mournful truth in Wordsworth's lines:

"The world is too much with us; late and soon,
    Getting and spending, we lay waste our powers."

Life is more than a matter of getting and spending. Of course Thoreau's teaching is no solution for the burning and social economic issues which with every month seem to be looming larger and larger. But the philosophy of Walden contains truths which just now are preeminently vital. During the war we learned that there were many supposed necessities with which we could do without and suffer no serious inconvenience. It was hoped that our national baptism of blood would cure us of our debauch of luxury. But still there are those to whom the recent years have brought more money than they ever dreamed of possessing. And wealth without a knowledge of how to use it is a curse. Every decade seems to wallow deeper and deeper in the mire of luxury. The severe and simple life of the fathers frequently is replaced by a soft and luxurious life on the part of the later generation. In the best sense of the word wealth is a national blessing, but there are circumstances where the proper name for it is what Ruskin terms "illth." No people has ever been able to endure an excess of luxury for any long period. Giving preeminence to "things" means the degradation of manhood and womanhood. Thoreau by reducing the material part of life to its simplest elements taught us a lesson which it would not be wise for us to forget.

"I have traveled much," said Thoreau, "in Concord." He himself lived not extensively but intensively. Men have journeyed around the world and have seen much less than that which this eccentric New Englander saw by the banks of Walden pond. Sometimes it would be much wiser for us to reread an old book than to make the acquaintance of a new one. Superficial study means shallow, loose-

thinking manhood and womanhood. Hum-
boldt unjustly spoke of an eminent American
writer as having traveled the farthest and seen
the least of any man in the world. The number of miles which a man covers means nothing.
What we bring back from a journey depends
upon what we take with us. To him that
hath shall be given. One truth studied from
all sides has in it more that is really educative
than a casual acquaintance with everything
beneath the sun. No sane man would to-day
repeat with reference to himself Bacon's never-
to-be-forgotten phrase: "I take all knowledge
to be my province." Range and breadth of
thought are poor substitutes for thoroughness
and depth. Agassiz would have a student
spend day after day upon the study of a
single fish. It is easy for a hurried, nervous
traveler to bring home nothing but a confused
mass of mental chaos. A renowned globe
trotter when interrogated in regard to Da
Vinci's Mona Lisa said that if the painting
were in the Louvre he must have seen it because he spent over three hours in that gallery. There are those who seem to have read
so much that they have forgotten everything.
Abraham Lincoln's lack of access to many
books was not an unmixed misfortune. What
he learned he learned. A man who knows one

village as Thoreau knew Concord and its environs is better educated than the professional wanderer upon the face of the earth. Most of us are satisfied to live upon the surface. Life becomes insipid because even though having eyes we see not.

Another great book is Gilbert White's The Parish of Selbourne, the result of an English clergyman's study of the natural history of a village and countryside. John Burroughs has found material for more than one idyll in and around an old hay barn. Jane Austin studied the commonplace lives of insignificant people and developed an unsurpassable power of analyzing the human mind and heart. The villager knows human nature better than the dweller in the city. His opportunities for an intensive study of his neighbors have been exceptionally good, and on account of the lack of other distractions he does not neglect to avail himself of his advantages along these lines. G. Stanley Hall once made the thought-provoking statement that all psychology has its origin in gossip. Thoreau found nature and life near at hand of such thrilling interest that he did not have to rush hither and yon in search of new excitement in order to prevent his life from becoming flat and inane.

It must not be thought, though, that Thoreau

was provincial-minded. He had spent four
years at Harvard, although he had not received his diploma on account of his refusing
to pay the fee demanded for the sheepskin,
his reason being that in his opinion it was not
worth the price. His professors did not know
what to make of the independent youth from
Concord. Yet his days at Cambridge were
not wasted. The quotations which are rather
generously scattered through his writings show
a wide and intelligent reading. His back-
ground was large enough to give a perspective
for the study of the life near at hand. He
was not like Goethe, who sat dreaming while
the guns of earth-shaking battles were boom-
ing around him. His patriotism, like everything else about him, was highly distinctive.
But he at least kept his finger upon the great
throbbing pulse of his time. Concord, however,
was the center of the world in which Thoreau
lived. Because he knew the life near at hand,
all that he said and wrote is singularly vital.
His feet were planted upon solid earth.

Life for all of us is made up of compromises.
No man, however sincere and noble his motives,
can do exactly as he pleases. Sometimes we
must take half of the loaf or go breadless.
But this was not the philosophy of Thoreau.
He was no compromiser. ⋅ No man conceded

less to society; yet no man was more loyal to his obligations to his fellowmen. He did his work as a surveyor with such faithfulness that those who followed him found his lines correct to the smallest detail. His philosophy of life was indeed one of "plain living and high thinking." He uttered truths to which his fellow countrymen still need to listen. There is no better way of raising the value of the fraction of a life than by decreasing the denominator.